THE NO TIME TO COOK BOOK

CONTENTS

Editorial
Food Editor Sheryle Eastwood
Assistant Food Editor Rachel Blackmore
Editorial Co-ordinator Margaret Kelly
Food Consultant Frances Naldrett
Sub Editor Ingaret Ward
Text Vicky Fraser
Nutrition Consultant Catherine Saxelby

Photography and Styling
Ashley Mackevicius
Wendy Berecry
Belinda Clayton

Design and Production
Sheridan Carter
Monica Kessler-Tay
Chris Hatcher

Publisher
Philippa Sandall

Published by J.B. Fairfax Press by arrangement with IPC Magazines Limited

The No Time To Cook Book
Includes Index
ISBN 1 86343 000 8

Typeset by Adtype, Sydney
Printed by Toppan Printing Co, Hong Kong
Distributed by J.B. Fairfax Press Ltd
9 Trinity Centre, Park Farm Estate
Wellingborough, Northants
Ph: (0933) 402330 Fax: (0933) 402234

Acknowledgements
The publishers would like to thank the following companies for their assistance during recipe testing and photography for this book:
Blanco Appliances, Knebel Kitchens, Leigh Mardon Pty Ltd, Master Foods of Australia, Meadow Lea Foods, Namco Cookware, Philips, Sunbeam Corporation Ltd, White Wings Foods.

INTRODUCTION

Find it hard to find time to cook?
Then this is the cookbook for you.
We show you how to enjoy the best of both worlds
with fast food and good eating.

☐ **Career?**
☐ **Young children?**
☐ **Busy schedule?**

The *No Time To Cook Book* has all the ingredients to help you combine the pleasure of nutritious, hassle-free home cooking with the pace of today's busy lifestyle. Now you can enjoy the best of both worlds with delicious meals prepared with the minimum of fuss. Just garnish with a sprig of tender loving care and you will have everything you need for enjoyable family fare and relaxing entertaining.

Every kitchen-tested recipe, is superbly photographed and captures the flavour and diversity of cooking today, using readily available ingredients and short cuts. You will find recipes for all occasions — appetising ideas for fast dinners when running late, easy, exotic stir-fries, tempting entrees and super side dishes.

There is also a great selection of healthy meals for hearty appetites, delicious desserts and tempting treats for picnics and barbecues. Enjoy nostalgic family favourites as well as luscious light meals that can be whipped up in minutes.

The *No Time To Cook Book* is not just a recipe book! Use it as your helping hand to beat the clock without compromising on quality. Right throughout the book there are practical hints and tips on food preparation, freezing, microwaving and cooking techniques that will help even the most experienced homemakers become whizzes in the kitchen.

When you want to try something new, make use of the step-by-step cooking class recipes (a feature of most chapters). This way you can perfect the technique of stuffing chicken thighs just under the skin as in Chicken with Spinach Ricotta and Lemon Filling, or filling snow peas with minted cream cheese, or removing all the bones from a whole fish before cooking.

CHECK-AND-GO

When planning a meal, use the easy Check-And-Go boxes which appear beside each ingredient. Simply check on your pantry shelf and if the ingredients are not there, tick the boxes as a reminder to add those items to your shopping list. To save time for busy cooks, ingredients have been kept to a minimum in all recipes and, where possible, convenience products used.

To ensure that you always have what you want on hand use the No Time To Shop Pantry Check List (page 76). This shopping list will keep your cupboards, refrigerator and freezer stocked with all the essentials plus a selection of interesting, easy-to-prepare foods.

POTATOES FILLED WITH
CHILLI BEANS

Serves 4

☑ 4 medium potatoes
☑ 310 g canned red kidney beans
☑ 1 tablespoon tomato paste
☐ 1-2 teaspoons chilli sauce
☐ paprika

TEN TIME SAVING TIPS

Try these tips in conjunction with our quick and easy recipes and you'll have extra time to relax!

1 Time saving starts with a well organised kitchen. Reorganising your kitchen, keeping the benchtops free and having all your utensils to hand makes life easier.

2 Tidy as you go, this not only speeds up preparation but saves time after the meal.

3 While you are busy in the kitchen, don't be reluctant to delegate, other people can help!

4 Plan a weekly menu and aim to shop once a week. Make the most of the No Time To Shop Pantry Check List at the back of the book and the Check-And-Go ingredients with every recipe.

5 Get to know your supermarket and write shopping lists according to the layout of the shelves.

6 Look for new and interesting convenience products such as pasta sauces and casserole bases. There are many good quality brands available and some are also low in salt, low in fat and high in fibre.

7 Make double quantities of your favourite soups, casseroles and sauces and freeze half for later.

8 Store frozen meals in containers that can go from freezer to microwave, to table and then to the dishwasher!

9 Buy products that are partly prepared — cubed meat, grated cheese, instant lasagne and boned chicken. Many greengrocers and supermarkets also prepare fresh salads and vegetable mixes for soups and casseroles.

10 When fruit is cheap, buy extra to stew and freeze for easy desserts or saucy toppings.

NO TIME TO FUSS PANTRY PLANNING

Try the following tips for no time to fuss pantry planning.

- Look in your cupboards and pull out all the jars of herbs, spices, jams, chutneys and whatever else is there. Start by throwing out all the products that have passed their Use By date. Next, out go the jars with one table-spoon of elderly jam or chutney left in them. Now make a list of those ingredi-ents you wish to replace and buy them next time you are shopping.

- If you store herbs and spices in alphabetical order, they are easily located and you can quickly see when they need replacing.

- Growing a few herbs of you own such as basil, coriander, rosemary, mint, chives and parsley means that you always have these on hand. These fresh herbs are often the secret to delicate flavours in meals.

- Place all staples, such as sugar and flour together. Store sauces and condiments according to favourite cuisines, just a glance in the cupboard will give you great ideas.

- Keep a good selection of frozen vegetables. Peas, beans, spinach and corn are great standbys and only take minutes to cook in the microwave.

- Keep a variety of breads and rolls in the freezer and defrost in the microwave for delicious instant sandwiches.

- Cooked pasta and rice freeze well, reheat in minutes in the microwave and save time on busy nights.

- Evaporated milk, available as full cream or skim milk, is a terrific standby when there is no fresh cream. It can be used for sauces and quiches and whips well when chilled. Store a few cans in the pantry for emergencies.

- Getting to know your local suppliers of meat, fish and chicken often means that they will suggest new and interest-ing foods for you to try. Don't be shy, ask "What's good this week?"

Blanco Appliances Knebel Kitchen

COOK'S TIP

Time saving starts with a well organised kitchen. Reorganising your kitchen, keeping the benchtops free and having all your utensils to hand makes life easier.

HOW TO MEASURE UP

In this book, fresh ingredients such as fish or meat are given in grams so you know how much to buy. A small, inexpensive set of kitchen scales is always handy and very easy to use.

Other ingredients in our recipes are given in tablespoons and cups, so you will need a nest of measuring cups (1 cup, $^1/_2$ cup, $^1/_3$ cup and $^1/_4$ cup); a set of spoons (1 tablespoon, 1 teaspoon, $^1/_2$ teaspoon and $^1/_4$ teaspoon): and a transparent graduated measuring jug (1 litre or 250 mL) for measuring liquids. Cup and spoon measures are level.

METRIC MEASURES

Cups	
$^1/_4$ cup	60 mL
$^1/_3$ cup	80 mL
$^1/_2$ cup	125 mL
1 cup	250 mL
Spoons	
$^1/_4$ teaspoon	1.25 mL
$^1/_2$ teaspoon	2.5 mL
1 teaspoon	5 mL
1 tablespoon	20 mL

QUICK METRIC IMPERIAL CONVERTER

g	oz	mL	fl.oz
30	1	30	1
60	2	60	2
125	4	125	4
250	8	250	8
370	12	370	12
500	16	500	16

OVEN TEMPERATURE

°C	°F	Gas Mark
120	250	$^1/_2$
150	300	2
180	350	4
220	425	7
240	475	8
250	500	9

Home Late
DINNER AT EIGHT

Walk in late and it's dinner at eight. Try these delicious ideas for family fare and effortless entertaining in under an hour.

CHEESE, SALAMI AND SPINACH STRUDEL

Serves 6

- ☐ **8 sheets filo pastry**
- ☐ **3 tablespoons olive oil**

FILLING
- ☐ **4 slices mozzarella cheese**
- ☐ **15 slices soft salami**
- ☐ **1/2 cup (125 mL) tomato sauce**
- ☐ **1/2 teaspoon dried sweet basil leaves**
- ☐ **6 spinach leaves, shredded**
- ☐ **1 egg, beaten**
- ☐ **320 g canned or bottled red capsicums, drained and sliced**
- ☐ **125 g pepperoni salami, skin removed and cut into thin slices**
- ☐ **20 stuffed olives, cut in half lengthways**
- ☐ **2 tablespoons grated Parmesan cheese**

1 Lay pastry sheets on top of each other, brushing between each layer with oil.
2 Place a layer of mozzarella evenly down the long edge of pastry, leaving about 5 cm at each end, top with rolled up soft salami. Pour over combined tomato sauce and basil. Arrange spinach over tomato sauce, top evenly with beaten egg. Place capsicum over spinach then top with a row each of pepperoni slices and olives.
3 Roll up tightly to enclose filling and tuck ends under. Transfer to an oven tray, brush with oil, sprinkle with Parmesan cheese and bake at 180°C for 30 minutes or until lightly browned. Serve sliced.

Watchpoint

When working with filo pastry, cover any sheets that are not immediately in use with a dampened tea towel, to prevent them from drying out.

PEPPERED ROAST WITH BRANDY CREAM SAUCE

Serves 4

- ☐ **1 piece rump steak, 4 cm thick and about 750 g in weight**
- ☐ **4 tablespoons cracked black peppercorns**
- ☐ **2 teaspoons polyunsaturated oil**

SAUCE
- ☐ **1/2 cup (125 mL) beef stock**
- ☐ **3 tablespoons dry white wine**
- ☐ **2 teaspoons brandy**
- ☐ **2 tablespoons cream**

1 Trim all visible fat from meat. Press both sides of steak into peppercorns.
2 Heat oil in a baking dish. Add meat and brown well on each side. Transfer to oven. Bake at 200°C for 30-35 minutes or until cooked as desired. Remove meat from dish and cover with aluminium foil. Stand 5 minutes before serving.
3 To make sauce, combine stock, wine and brandy and pour into baking dish. Stir over medium heat for 2-3 minutes lifting sediment from base of dish. Remove from heat and whisk in cream. Slice steak, spoon over sauce and serve.

Microwave It

Prepare ingredients. Preheat browning dish on HIGH (100%) 7 minutes. Cook oil and steak on MEDIUM/HIGH (70%) 10 minutes. Remove from dish and stand covered 10 minutes. Combine stock, wine and brandy. Pour into browning dish. Cook on HIGH (100%) 2-3 minutes, stirring during cooking.

Cheese, Salami and Spinach Strudel, Peppered Roast with Brandy Cream Sauce and Ham Steaks with Cranberry Sauce (see page 8)

Plates Pillivuyt, Hale Imports *Document Case* Made Where

As we see it,
long-held dislikes
have been weakened

SPICY MEATLOAF WITH CRUNCHY CHEESE TOPPING

Serves 4

- ☐ **500 g lean minced lamb**
- ☐ **2 tablespoons (or 35 g packet) taco seasoning mix**
- ☐ **1 egg**
- ☐ **$^3/_4$ cup (50 g) soft breadcrumbs**
- ☐ **1 cup (125 g) grated tasty cheese**
- ☐ **1 cup (250 mL) taco sauce**
- ☐ **25 g packet corn chips**

1 Combine meat, seasoning mix, egg and breadcrumbs. Press half of the mixture into a 20 cm x 13 cm loaf pan. Top with $^3/_4$ cup cheese, then cover with remaining meat mixture. Cook at 180°C for 40-45 minutes. Drain off any liquid, cover and allow to stand for 10 minutes.

2 Turn meatloaf out onto an ovenproof plate. Brush surface liberally with taco sauce, top with remaining cheese and crushed corn chips. Cook at 200°C for 10 minutes or until cheese has melted. Serve sliced, hot or cold.

MICROWAVE IT

Prepare as above. Arrange in a 20 cm x 13 cm microwave loaf pan. Cook on MEDIUM/HIGH (70%) for 15 minutes. Add topping as above. Cook on HIGH (100%) for 3 minutes or until cheese has melted.

HAM STEAKS WITH CRANBERRY SAUCE

If you prefer, substitute cream cheese or ricotta cheese for the cottage cheese.

Serves 4

- ☐ **15 g butter**
- ☐ **4 ham steaks**

CRANBERRY SAUCE

- ☐ **$^1/_2$ cup (125 mL) cranberry sauce**
- ☐ **3 tablespoons red currant jelly**
- ☐ **1 tablespoon port, optional**

TOPPING

- ☐ **250 g cottage cheese**
- ☐ **2 shallots, finely chopped**
- ☐ **1 cup (50 g) alfalfa sprouts**

1 Melt butter in pan and cook ham steaks over medium heat for 1-2 minutes each side. Remove from pan and keep warm.

2 To make sauce, combine cranberry sauce, red currant jelly and port in the pan. Stir over low heat until well mixed.

3 Combine cottage cheese and shallots. Top each steak with sprouts and cottage cheese mixture and spoon over cranberry sauce to serve.

Plates The Design Store *Tiles* Pazotti Tiles

Crab and Asparagus Puffs and Golden Oat Fish Fillets

Plates Pillivuyt, Hale Imports *Tiles* Country Floors

Spicy Meatloaf with Crunchy Cheese Topping

CRAB AND ASPARAGUS PUFFS

Serves 4

- ☐ **4 pita bread rounds**
- ☐ **4 slices shoulder ham**
- ☐ **340 g canned asparagus spears, drained**
- ☐ **155 g canned crabmeat, drained**
- ☐ **2 egg whites, stiffly beaten**
- ☐ **2 tablespoons mayonnaise**
- ☐ **2 teaspoons sweet chilli sauce**

1 Place pita rounds on a lightly greased oven tray. Top each with a slice of ham, some asparagus and crabmeat.

2 Combine stiffly beaten egg whites, mayonnaise and chilli sauce and spoon over each round. Bake at 220°C for 10 minutes or until puffed and golden. Serve immediately.

COOK'S TIP

Pita or Lebanese bread is available at larger supermarkets and delicatessens. Delicious with salads and sandwich toppings, it also makes an easy base for quick pizzas.

GOLDEN OAT FISH FILLETS

This recipe can be made with any white-fleshed fish, such as perch, sole, halibut or hake. Lemon pepper seasoning is a mixture of pepper, salt, sugar, lemon peel and lemon extract.

Serves 4

- ☐ **3 tablespoons fine oatmeal**
- ☐ **1/2 cup (50 g) rolled oats**
- ☐ **3/4 cup (50 g) soft breadcrumbs**
- ☐ **1/2 teaspoon lemon pepper**
- ☐ **plain flour**
- ☐ **1 egg, beaten**
- ☐ **4 fish fillets**
- ☐ **30 g butter**
- ☐ **1 tablespoon oil**
- ☐ **lemon wedges**

1 Combine oatmeal, oats, breadcrumbs and pepper. Coat fish with flour, dip in beaten egg and coat well with crumb mixture.

2 Heat butter and oil in a frypan, cook fish until golden brown on both sides. Serve with lemon wedges.

STEP-BY-STEP

CHICKEN WITH SPINACH RICOTTA AND LEMON FILLING

If Chicken Marylands are unavailable, you can substitute drum sticks or thighs. If you prefer, substitute cottage cheese for ricotta and fresh spinach in place of frozen.

Serves 4

- ☐ **4 chicken Marylands (leg and thigh joints)**

FILLING

- ☐ **125 g frozen spinach, thawed**
- ☐ **1 teaspoon minced garlic**
- ☐ **125 g ricotta cheese**
- ☐ **2 teaspoons grated Parmesan cheese**
- ☐ **1 teaspoon grated lemon rind**
- ☐ **ground nutmeg**
- ☐ **30 g butter, melted**

SAUCE

- ☐ **310 g canned tomato puree**
- ☐ **2 teaspoons Worcestershire sauce**

1 Squeeze spinach to remove excess liquid and combine with garlic, ricotta, Parmesan, lemon rind and pinch nutmeg.

2 Loosen skin on chicken with fingers. Push spinach filling gently under skin down to the drumstick. Arrange Marylands in an ovenproof dish, brush with melted butter and bake at 180°C for 35-40 minutes.

3 To make the sauce, combine tomato puree and Worcestershire sauce in saucepan and simmer gently for 3-4 minutes. Spoon sauce over chicken and serve.

Squeeze excess moisture from spinach. Combine with other filling ingredients

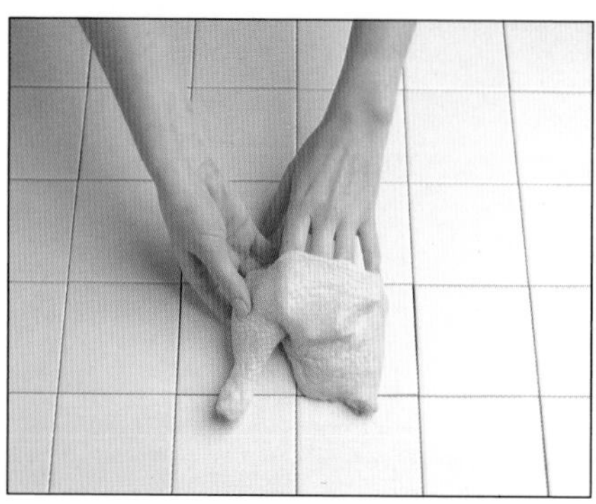

Loosen skin on chicken using fingers

Push spinach filling gently under skin

Chicken with Spinach Ricotta and Lemon Filling

Plates Mid City Home and Garden *Tray* Accoutrement

Plates The Design Store *Tiles* Country Floors

Steak with French Mustard Sauce and Marinated Sate Chicken Wings

STEAK WITH FRENCH MUSTARD SAUCE

Serves 4

- ☐ **4 lean rib eye steaks (scotch fillet)**
- ☐ **30 g butter**

FRENCH MUSTARD SAUCE

- ☐ **2 shallots, finely chopped**
- ☐ **1 tablespoon wholegrain mustard**
- ☐ **2 teaspoons French mustard**
- ☐ **$^1/_2$ cup (125 mL) dry white wine**
- ☐ **3 tablespoons water**
- ☐ **1 teaspoon honey**
- ☐ **$^1/_4$ teaspoon dried thyme**
- ☐ **2 tablespoons cream or evaporated skim milk**
- ☐ **1$^1/_2$ tablespoons grated tasty cheese**

1 Trim meat of all visible fat. Melt butter in frypan, cook steaks for 4-5 minutes each side. Remove from pan and keep warm.

2 To make sauce, add shallots to pan and saute for 1 minute. Stir in combined mustards, wine, water, honey and thyme. Cook over medium heat for 3-4 minutes until sauce has reduced slightly.

3 Remove pan from heat and stir in cream and cheese. Spoon sauce over steaks and serve.

MARINATED SATE CHICKEN WINGS

Sate sauce is a spicy peanut sauce available in supermarkets. To make your own, combine 1 tablespoon smooth peanut butter, 1 tablespoon soy sauce, $^1/_2$ teaspoon crushed garlic, 1 teaspoon lemon juice and a pinch of chilli powder.

Serves 4

- ☐ **750 g chicken wings**

MARINADE

- ☐ **$^1/_4$ teaspoon five spice powder**
- ☐ **$^1/_4$ teaspoon chilli powder**
- ☐ **2 tablespoons sate sauce**
- ☐ **$^1/_2$ teaspoon curry powder**
- ☐ **1 teaspoon cornflour**
- ☐ **$^1/_2$ teaspoon sugar**
- ☐ **1 teaspoon oyster sauce**
- ☐ **2 tablespoons dry white wine**
- ☐ **3 tablespoons oil**
- ☐ **3 medium onions, cut into eighths**
- ☐ **2 teaspoons grated fresh ginger**

1 Combine chicken wings with five spice powder, chilli powder, sate sauce, curry powder, cornflour, sugar, oyster sauce and white wine. Allow to stand for at least 10-15 minutes to absorb flavour. Drain, reserving marinade.

2 Heat 1 tablespoon oil in frypan or wok. Add onions and ginger and saute 2-3 minutes until onion is transparent. Remove from pan and set aside.

3 Heat remaining oil. Add chicken wings and cook over high heat until well browned on both sides. Reduce heat and cook a further 10-15 minutes until tender. Return onions and ginger to pan and pour over reserved marinade. Toss over high heat for 2-3 minutes or until sauce boils.

COOK'S TIP

Marinating chicken or meat in a mixture containing wine, soy sauce, fruit juice and herbs or spices will tenderise the meat and add flavour. Marinate the meat or chicken in a glass or plastic bowl for at least one hour. But, for really tasty, succulent results, marinate covered overnight in the refrigerator.

Flan Pillivuyt, Hale Imports

Cook's Tip

Precious time can be saved by keeping cooked rice or pasta in the refrigerator or freezer. 1 cup of uncooked rice makes 3 cups of cooked rice.

Try "cooking" rice while you are at work with this easy tip. Place 1 cup of quick cooking brown rice in a heatproof bowl with 2 cups of boiling water. Cover with plastic food wrap and set aside. When you return home, your rice will be ready to use. This method is not suitable for short or long grain white rice or for natural brown rice.

Ham Cheese and Leek Pie

Tangy Lamb with Mushroom and Tomato Sauce and Honey Pork Kebabs

Plates Pillivuyt, Hale Imports *Tiles* Pazotti Tiles

HAM CHEESE AND LEEK PIE

Serves 6

- ☐ **15 g butter**
- ☐ **2 leeks, washed, trimmed and sliced**
- ☐ **3 cups (500 g) cooked brown rice**
- ☐ **4 slices ham, chopped**
- ☐ **5 eggs**
- ☐ **2 cups (500 mL) milk**
- ☐ **$^{1}/_{2}$ cup (60 g) grated tasty cheese**
- ☐ **1 tablespoon chopped fresh parsley**

1 Melt butter in frypan, saute leeks for 3-4 minutes or until soft. Fold through rice and spoon into a lightly greased 27 cm ovenproof pie dish. Arrange ham over top.

2 Whisk together eggs and milk and season to taste. Pour over rice, sprinkle with cheese and parsley. Bake at 190°C for 25 minutes until the top is firm and golden.

TANGY LAMB WITH MUSHROOM AND TOMATO SAUCE

In this very versatile recipe, you can substitute a variety of vegetables such as celery, zucchini or carrots depending on what you have or to your taste.

Serves 4

- ☐ **4 lean lamb leg steaks**
- ☐ **2 teaspoons polyunsaturated oil**

MUSHROOM AND TOMATO SAUCE
- ☐ **1 small onion, chopped**
- ☐ **1 clove garlic, crushed**
- ☐ **120 g mushrooms, sliced**
- ☐ **440 g canned tomatoes**
- ☐ **1 tablespoon chopped fresh parsley**
- ☐ **$^1/_2$ teaspoon dried rosemary**
- ☐ **$^1/_2$ teaspoon dried sweet basil leaves**
- ☐ **$^1/_2$ teaspoon sugar**
- ☐ **3 tablespoons chicken stock**

1 Trim all visible fat from meat. Heat oil in a frypan and cook steaks for 1-2 minutes each side. Remove from pan.

2 To make sauce, add onion, garlic and mushrooms to pan. Cook for 2-3 minutes. Stir in mashed undrained tomatoes, parsley, rosemary, basil, sugar and stock. Return steaks to pan and simmer uncovered for 10 minutes.

HONEY PORK KEBABS

Substitute chicken or seafood for pork if you wish. An easy way to shred cabbage quickly is to cut it into halves then into quarters, work with one quarter at a time and shred finely. One quarter of a medium cabbage will give you about $1^1/_2$ cups of shredded cabbage.

Serves 4

- ☐ **500 g pork fillets**
- ☐ **125 g button mushrooms**
- ☐ **8 small onions, peeled**
- ☐ **$^1/_2$ red capsicum, cubed**
- ☐ **$^1/_2$ green capsicum, cubed**
- ☐ **1 orange, segmented**
- ☐ **$^1/_2$ small cabbage, finely shredded**
- ☐ **juice 1 orange**

BASTE
- ☐ **2 tablespoons warmed honey**
- ☐ **3 teaspoons polyunsaturated oil**
- ☐ **few drops sesame oil**
- ☐ **$1^1/_2$ tablespoons lemon juice**

1 Cut pork into 2 cm cubes. Thread onto eight oiled bamboo skewers, alternating with mushrooms, onions and capsicum. Toss orange segments with cabbage and orange juice and chill.

2 Combine honey with oils and lemon juice and brush over kebabs. Grill kebabs for 8-10 minutes, turning and brushing frequently with baste, as they cook. Serve the kebabs on pita bread with cabbage and orange salad.

STIR UP A MEAL
IN MINUTES

Stir-fry gourmet meals in minutes with this exciting variety of dishes that bring an exotic touch to the family table.

STIR-FRY VEGETABLES WITH MANGO AND CASHEWS

Serves 6

- ☐ **2 tablespoons polyunsaturated oil**
- ☐ **2 onions, cut into eighths**
- ☐ **2 carrots, cut into thin strips**
- ☐ **2 stalks celery, cut into thin strips**
- ☐ **2 teaspoons turmeric**
- ☐ **2 cloves garlic, crushed**
- ☐ **6 shallots, chopped**
- ☐ **2 tablespoons white vinegar**
- ☐ **2 tablespoons sugar**
- ☐ **1 mango, peeled and sliced**
- ☐ **125 g snow peas, trimmed**
- ☐ **$^{3}/_{4}$ cup (190 mL) chicken stock**
- ☐ **125 g roasted unsalted cashews**

1 Heat oil in a frypan or wok. Add onions, carrots, celery. Stir-fry until lightly browned. Stir in combined turmeric, garlic, shallots, vinegar and sugar.
2 Add mango, snow peas, stock. Stir-fry 5 minutes until vegetables are tender. Fold through cashew nuts and serve.

HOT SPICY PORK

Serves 6

- ☐ **1 kg pork fillet, cut into thin strips**
- ☐ **2 tablespoons cornflour**
- ☐ **$^{1}/_{2}$ teaspoon five spice powder**
- ☐ **2 tablespoons polyunsaturated oil**
- ☐ **1 teaspoon grated fresh ginger**
- ☐ **2 tablespoons honey**
- ☐ **2 teaspoons cornflour blended with 4 tablespoons water**
- ☐ **2 teaspoons hot chilli sauce**
- ☐ **2 teaspoons oyster sauce**
- ☐ **4 tablespoons lemon juice**

1 Toss meat strips in combined cornflour and five spice powder. Heat oil in a frypan or wok and stir-fry pork mixture over high heat for 3-4 minutes until pork is well browned.
2 Add grated ginger and honey to pan and cook gently for 1 minute. Pour in blended cornflour, chilli sauce, oyster sauce and lemon juice. Stir until sauce boils and thickens. Serve immediately.

COOK'S TIP

Slice meat or poultry across the grain in approximately $^{1}/_{2}$ cm wide strips. This ensures a more tender result when cooked.

CHICKEN AND SNOW PEAS WITH PASTA

Serves 4

- ☐ **500 g wholemeal spiral pasta**
- ☐ **2 tablespoons polyunsaturated oil**
- ☐ **150 g snow peas, trimmed**
- ☐ **1 clove garlic, crushed**
- ☐ **1 small fresh red chilli, finely chopped**
- ☐ **250 g chopped cooked chicken**
- ☐ **1 tablespoon cornflour, blended in 3 tablespoons chicken stock**
- ☐ **2 tablespoons soy sauce**
- ☐ **3 tablespoons dry sherry**

1 Bring a large saucepan of water to the boil and cook pasta following the packet instructions. Drain and set aside.
2 Heat oil in a frypan or wok. Add snow peas, garlic and chilli and stir-fry for 1 minute. Add chicken and stir-fry for 2 minutes. Toss in cooked pasta, blended cornflour, soy sauce and sherry. Heat through, stirring constantly until sauce boils and thickens. Serve immediately.

Plates Villa Italiana

Stir-fry Vegetables with Mango and Cashews, Hot Spicy Pork and Chicken and Snow Peas with Pasta

Cook's Tip

There is no need to wait for the mango season as you can use canned mangoes if fresh ones are unavailable.

Plates Pillivuyt, Hale Imports

ORIENTAL LAMB AND SPINACH

Serves 4

- ☐ **500 g lean lamb leg steaks, cut into thin slices**
- ☐ **2 tablespoons oyster sauce**
- ☐ **2 tablespoons dry white wine**
- ☐ **1 teaspoon sugar**
- ☐ **1/2 teaspoon sesame oil**
- ☐ **1 bunch spinach, washed**
- ☐ **2 teaspoons grated fresh ginger**
- ☐ **2 tablespoons polyunsaturated oil**
- ☐ **1/2 teaspoon cornflour blended with 3 tablespoons chicken stock**

1 Combine meat with oyster sauce, wine, sugar and sesame oil. Wash spinach and remove thick white stalks, cut into 2.5 cm slices then cut leaves into large pieces.

2 Heat oil in frypan or wok. Stir-fry meat in two batches for 2-3 minutes each batch until meat browns. Remove and set aside. Add spinach stalks and ginger to pan and cook gently for 3 minutes. Return meat to pan and stir in spinach leaves.

3 Pour in blended cornflour and toss over high heat for 3-4 minutes until spinach has softened.

> **COOK'S TIP**
> Substituting chicken fillets or pork fillets for the lamb makes a change.

RED PEPPERED BEEF

This recipe is delicious served with rice or noodles.

Serves 4

- ☐ **500 g rump steak, cut into thin strips**
- ☐ **2 teaspoons cornflour**
- ☐ **4 tablespoons soy sauce**
- ☐ **3 tablespoons polyunsaturated oil**
- ☐ **2 red capsicums, cut into thin strips**
- ☐ **1 small red chilli, finely chopped**
- ☐ **3 shallots, cut into 5 cm lengths**
- ☐ **1 clove garlic, crushed**
- ☐ **2 teaspoons grated fresh ginger**
- ☐ **1 teaspoon sugar**
- ☐ **2 tablespoons dry sherry**

1 Sprinkle meat strips with cornflour and 2 tablespoons soy sauce. Toss to coat and leave for 5 minutes.

Oriental Lamb and Spinach, Red Peppered Beef and Tangy Lemon Chicken

Spoon Pillivuyt, Hale Imports

Abalone and Fried Rice

2 Heat 1 tablespoon oil in a frypan or wok, add capsicums, chilli, shallots, garlic and ginger and cook for 2-3 minutes. Remove from pan and set aside.

3 Heat remaining oil and stir-fry meat for 2-3 minutes. Return capsicum mixture to the pan. Combine remaining soy sauce, sugar and sherry. Pour in pan and stir-fry a further minute to heat through.

> **COOK'S TIP**
>
> Never scour your wok when washing as this will cause the food to stick the next time you use it.
>
> The best way to clean your wok is to wash it in warm soapy water using a soft cloth. Then rinse thoroughly in plenty of hot running water. Wipe dry with absorbent paper towel. It is a good idea to oil your wok lightly before you put it away. This will keep your wok well seasoned.

ABALONE AND FRIED RICE

Abalone requires very little cooking. If you cook it for more than 1-2 minutes, it will turn into something resembling shoe leather, so be careful. Canned abalone only requires gentle heating through.

Serves 4

- ☐ **2 tablespoons polyunsaturated oil**
- ☐ **1 onion, grated**
- ☐ **2 eggs, beaten**
- ☐ **3 cups (460 g) cooked long-grain rice**
- ☐ **450 g canned abalone, drained**
- ☐ **6 shallots, chopped**
- ☐ **1 tablespoon soy sauce**

1 Heat 1 tablespoon oil in frypan or wok. Cook onion until soft. Pour in beaten eggs, swirling to coat base of pan and cook until set. Remove and cut onion omelette into large strips.

2 Heat remaining oil in pan. Toss in rice, abalone and shallots and stir-fry for only 2 minutes. Fold in egg slices and sprinkle soy sauce over. Stir-fry for a further minute. Serve immediately.

TANGY LEMON CHICKEN

Serves 4

- ☐ **1 medium cooked chicken**
- ☐ **2 tablespoons polyunsaturated oil**
- ☐ **2 teaspoons grated fresh ginger**
- ☐ **3 tablespoons lemon juice**
- ☐ **1 cup (250 mL) chicken stock**
- ☐ **1½ tablespoons honey**
- ☐ **2 tablespoons sugar**
- ☐ **1 tablespoon cornflour blended with 1 tablespoon water**
- ☐ **2 shallots, chopped**

1 Cut chicken into serving pieces. Heat oil in frypan or wok and stir-fry chicken for 2-3 minutes. Remove, set aside and keep warm.

2 Stir in ginger and cook for 1 minute. Pour in combined lemon juice, stock, honey and sugar. Add blended cornflour to pan and cook for 1-2 minutes until the sauce has thickened.

3 Return chicken to pan and heat through gently. Serve sprinkled with shallots.

STEP-BY-STEP

SEAFOOD WITH MANGOES

Serves 4

- ☐ **250 g squid**
- ☐ **250 g green king prawns**
- ☐ **250 g scallops**
- ☐ **$^{1}/_{4}$ teaspoon sugar**
- ☐ **1 teaspoon cornflour**
- ☐ **2 tablespoons polyunsaturated oil**
- ☐ **425 g canned sliced mangoes, drained and cut into 1 cm strips**
- ☐ **6 shallots, cut into 1 cm diagonal slices**
- ☐ **2 teaspoons grated fresh ginger**

SAUCE

- ☐ **2 teaspoons cornflour blended with $^{3}/_{4}$ cup (190 mL) chicken stock**
- ☐ **2 tablespoons dry white wine**
- ☐ **1 tablespoon soy sauce**
- ☐ **1 teaspoon sesame oil**
- ☐ **2 tablespoons white vinegar**
- ☐ **2 teaspoons sugar**

1 Clean squid and cut into halves, spread out flat with inside facing up. Mark in diamond pattern with a sharp knife, then cut into diagonal pieces. Shell and devein prawns. Combine squid, prawns and scallops with sugar and cornflour.

2 Heat oil in frypan or wok. Stir-fry seafood for 2-3 minutes until just tender. Remove and set aside. Add ginger to pan and stir-fry for 1 minute.

3 Combine blended cornflour with wine, soy sauce, sesame oil, vinegar and sugar. Pour into pan and stir until sauce is boiling. Reduce heat and simmer for 3 minutes. Return seafood to pan with mangoes and shallots. Toss for 2-3 minutes until heated through.

Seafood with Mangoes

Clean squid

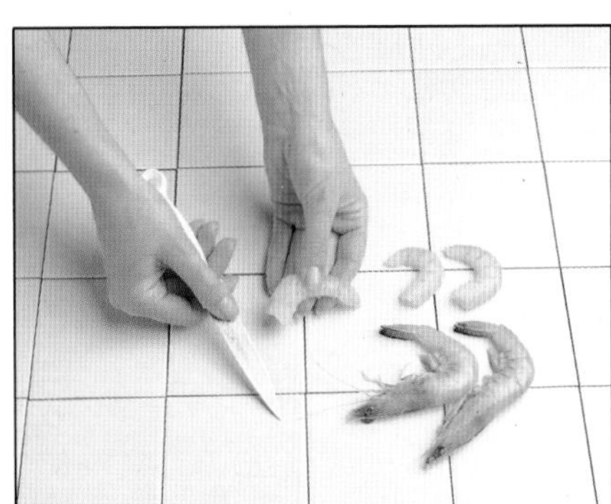

Shell and devein prawns

Return seafood to pan with mangoes and shallots

SQUID

To prepare squid, pull away tentacles and intestines from body. Pull feather out of the body and discard. Cut the tentacles from intestines and discard intestines. Rinse the body and tentacles under cold-running water and peel skin away from the body. Drain well and pat dry on absorbent paper. Halve the bodies lengthwise and score the surface with a sharp knife in a diamond pattern.

Squid is also known as cuttlefish or calamari and can be prepared as above in pieces or cut into rings to cook.

Like all seafood, squid only requires minimal cooking. Overcooking will cause toughness.

Super Sides And GREAT BEGINNINGS

Easy entrees and side dishes that perfectly complement a main course are a must for the busy cook. Surprise family and friends with these tasty combinations.

AVOCADO WITH SALMON AND CRAB

Serves 4

- ☐ **2 large avocados**
- ☐ **100g crab pieces, flaked**
- ☐ **4 slices smoked salmon, chopped**
- ☐ **3 tablespoons cream**
- ☐ **2 teaspoons mayonnaise**
- ☐ **1 tablespoon tomato sauce**
- ☐ **2-3 dashes Tabasco sauce**
- ☐ **2 teaspoons lemon juice**

1 Scoop the flesh from one of the avocados. Chop and combine with crab and salmon. Cut the remaining avocado into quarters and remove the stone. Spoon mixture into the hollow left by the stone.
2 Combine cream, mayonnaise, tomato sauce, Tabasco and lemon juice and spoon over filled avocado.

MANDARIN SMOKED CHICKEN AND SNOW PEA SALAD

Serves 4

- ☐ **250 g snow peas, trimmed**
- ☐ **400 g chopped smoked chicken**
- ☐ **300 g canned mandarin segments, drained**
- ☐ **1 cup (50 g) bean sprouts**
- ☐ **110 g canned water chestnuts, drained and thinly sliced**

DRESSING

- ☐ **4 tablespoons polyunsaturated oil**
- ☐ **1 tablespoon white wine vinegar**
- ☐ **$^1/_2$ teaspoon French mustard**

1 Drop snow peas into a saucepan of boiling water. Cook for 1 minute. Drain and refresh under cold running water. Pat dry on absorbent paper.
2 Combine snow peas with chicken, mandarins, bean sprouts and water chestnuts in a serving dish.
3 To make dressing, combine oil, vinegar and mustard in a screw top jar. Shake until well mixed. Pour dressing over salad and serve.

PUMPKIN AND APPLE SOUP

Serves 4

- ☐ **500 g pumpkin, peeled and chopped**
- ☐ **1 large carrot, peeled and chopped**
- ☐ **1 large cooking apple, peeled and chopped**
- ☐ **1 tablespoon chopped fresh mint**
- ☐ **$^1/_2$ teaspoon mixed spice**
- ☐ **$^1/_2$ teaspoon ground nutmeg**
- ☐ **1 teaspoon cracked black peppercorns**
- ☐ **2 cups (500 mL) chicken stock**
- ☐ **30 g butter**
- ☐ **3 tablespoons cream or evaporated skim milk**

1 Place pumpkin, carrot, apple, mint, mixed spice, nutmeg, peppercorns and stock in a large saucepan. Dot with butter, cover and cook over medium heat for 20 minutes until pumpkin is tender.
2 Puree in a blender or processor until smooth. Stir in cream and serve.

> **MICROWAVE IT**
>
> This soup is easily made in the microwave, just place the vegetables, spices and stock in a microwave safe bowl, cover and cook on HIGH (100%) for 15-16 minutes or until vegetables are tender. Puree, stir in cream and serve.

Plates and Spoons Villeroy & Boch

Avocado with Salmon and Crab, Mandarin Smoked Chicken and Snow Pea Salad and Pumpkin and Apple Soup

Bowls Pillivuyt, Hale Imports *Tiles* Country Floors

CHICKEN AND AVOCADO SOUP

This soup can also be quickly and easily made in the microwave.

Serves 4

- ☐ **1 onion, finely chopped**
- ☐ **15 g butter**
- ☐ **1 large potato, peeled and diced**
- ☐ **3 1/2 cups (875 mL) chicken stock**
- ☐ **310 g canned corn kernels, drained**
- ☐ **400 g cooked chicken, chopped**
- ☐ **1 teaspoon cracked black peppercorns**
- ☐ **3 tablespoons cream or evaporated skim milk**
- ☐ **1 avocado, peeled, stoned and diced**

1 Place onion and butter in a large saucepan. Cook for 2-3 minutes. Stir in potato and stock. Cover and cook over medium heat for 15-20 minutes or until potato is tender.

2 Add corn, chicken and pepper. Cook 5-6 minutes until heated through. Spoon soup into individual serving dishes. Swirl in cream and top with diced avocado.

QUICK SEAFOOD SOUP

Serves 4

- ☐ **4 fish fillets**
- ☐ **30 g butter**
- ☐ **2 leeks, washed and sliced**
- ☐ **12 oysters**
- ☐ **250 g cooked mussels, drained**
- ☐ **440 g canned peeled tomatoes, mashed with liquid**
- ☐ **3 1/2 cups (875 mL) chicken stock**
- ☐ **2 tablespoons tomato paste**
- ☐ **1 tablespoon chopped fresh basil**
- ☐ **1/2 teaspoon brown sugar**

1 Remove skin and bones from fish and cut flesh into pieces. Melt butter in a large saucepan and cook leeks for 2 minutes.

2 Stir in fish, oysters, mussels, tomatoes, stock, paste, basil and sugar and season to taste. Simmer for 5-10 minutes or until fish is cooked

Chicken and Avocado Soup and Quick Seafood Soup

Plate Villeroy & Boch

Snow Pea Boats with Minted Cream Cheese

Drop snow peas into boiling water

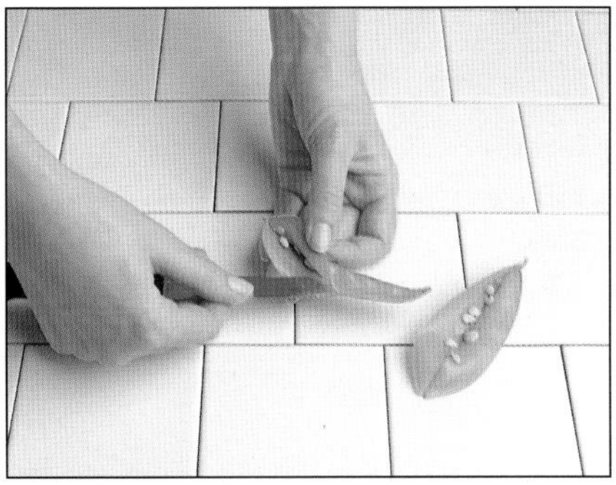

Slit with a sharp knife or scissors

Cook's Tip

Snow peas (sometimes called mangetout) are an edible pod pea. To prepare for cooking, top and tail with a sharp knife and pull away strings from older, larger peas. Snow peas can be steamed, boiled, microwaved or stir-fried.

Pipe cream cheese into snow peas

STEP-BY-STEP

SNOW PEA BOATS WITH MINTED CREAM CHEESE

Serves 6

- ☐ **18 snow peas, trimmed**
- ☐ **125 g packet cream cheese**
- ☐ **30 g butter**
- ☐ **1 cup (50 g) fresh mint leaves, finely chopped**
- ☐ **1 teaspoon sugar**
- ☐ **1 teaspoon horseradish relish**

1 Drop snow peas into a saucepan of boiling water and cook for 1 minute. Drain and refresh under cold running water. Pat dry on absorbent paper.

2 Beat cream cheese and butter together until smooth. Add mint, sugar and horseradish. Slit snow peas on one edge with a sharp knife or scissors. Spoon or pipe cream cheese mixture into snow peas. Refrigerate until firm.

FRENCH ONION FLANS

Serves 6

- ☐ **3 sheets prepared puff pastry, thawed**
- ☐ **6 onions, sliced**
- ☐ **60 g butter**
- ☐ **3 eggs, beaten**
- ☐ **1 $^{3}/_{4}$ cups (435 g) sour cream**
- ☐ **1 teaspoon ground nutmeg**
- ☐ **1$^{1}/_{2}$ teaspoons horseradish relish**
- ☐ **1$^{1}/_{2}$ cups (175 g) grated tasty cheese**

1 Line six individual flan tins with pastry. Melt butter in a frypan and cook onions until golden. Divide into six portions and spread over base of flans.

2 Combine eggs, sour cream, nutmeg and horseradish. Pour into flans. Top with cheese and bake at 200°C for 20 minutes or until firm.

COOK'S TIP

To keep egg yolks fresh, cover with water and store in the refrigerator. When baking, have eggs at room temperature to gain maximum volume.

ASPARAGUS WITH CREAMY VERMOUTH SAUCE

Serves 4

- ☐ **2 bunches asparagus**

SAUCE

- ☐ **3 tablespoons dry vermouth**
- ☐ **3 tablespoons water**
- ☐ **1 tablespoon chopped fresh dill leaves**
- ☐ **2 teaspoons lemon juice**
- ☐ **1 teaspoon sugar**
- ☐ **2 teaspoons cornflour blended with 3 tablespoons cream**

1 Trim ends of asparagus. Drop into a frypan of boiling water. Cook for 5 minutes or until tender. Drain and keep warm.

2 To make sauce, combine vermouth, water, dill, lemon juice and sugar in a pan, and bring to the boil. Reduce heat and simmer for 4 minutes. Whisk in blended cornflour. Stir over heat until sauce thickens. Arrange asparagus on a serving plate, spoon sauce over and serve.

French Onion Flans and Asparagus with Creamy Vermouth Sauce

Plates Pillivuyt, Hale Imports

COOK'S TIP

If fresh dill is unavailable, substitute 1 teaspoon dried dill leaves or $^{1}/_{4}$ teaspoon ground dill.

Camembert Surprise with Banana Sauce

CAMEMBERT SURPRISE WITH BANANA SAUCE

Serves 4

- ☐ **4 x 125 g Camembert cheese**
- ☐ **2 ripe bananas, peeled and sliced**
- ☐ **lemon juice**
- ☐ **2 teaspoons desiccated coconut**
- ☐ **plain flour**
- ☐ **1 egg, beaten**
- ☐ **3 tablespoons milk**
- ☐ **3 cups (375 g) dry breadcrumbs**
- ☐ **polyunsaturated oil for cooking**

BANANA SAUCE

- ☐ **2 ripe bananas**
- ☐ **$^1/_2$ cup (125 mL) coconut cream**
- ☐ **2 tablespoons cream**
- ☐ **$^1/_4$ teaspoon ground mixed spice**
- ☐ **1 teaspoon lemon juice**

1 Halve Camemberts horizontally. Sprinkle banana slices with lemon juice and arrange on four of the Camembert halves. Sprinkle with coconut and top with remaining cheese halves. Press together firmly.

2 Combine egg and milk. Dip each Camembert in flour, egg mixture and breadcrumbs. Repeat crumbing process. Chill until firm.

3 Cook in hot oil until golden. Drain on absorbent paper and serve with sauce.

4 To prepare sauce, peel and roughly chop bananas. Place into the bowl of a food processor, add coconut cream, cream, spice and lemon juice. Process until smooth. Serve sauce separately or spooned over Camembert.

Cook's Tip

Use a toothpick to hold each Camembert together while preparing and cooking. Remove toothpick before serving.

POTATO NEST WITH CARROT PUREE

For something different try using sweet potatoes in place of the potatoes in this recipe, accompany them with parsnip puree and substitute lemon juice for the orange juice.

Serves 6

NEST
- ☐ **4 large potatoes, peeled**
- ☐ **2 egg yolks**
- ☐ **1/4 teaspoon nutmeg**
- ☐ **60 g butter**

CARROT PUREE
- ☐ **6 large carrots**
- ☐ **3/4 cup (190 mL) chicken stock**
- ☐ **2 tablespoons orange juice**
- ☐ **1/4 teaspoon ground nutmeg**

1 To make nest, cook potatoes in a saucepan of boiling water until tender. Drain and return to pan. Toss over heat for 2-3 minutes to dry. Remove from heat and mash well. Stir in egg yolks, nutmeg and half the butter. Season to taste.

2 Spoon mixture into a piping bag and pipe a decorative border around the edge of an ovenproof dinner plate. Spoon any leftover potato into the centre of plate. Brush with remaining melted butter and bake at 180°C for 20 minutes.

3 To make puree, place carrots and stock in a saucepan, bring to the boil, and simmer covered for 10 minutes or until carrots are tender. Cool slightly. Puree carrot mixture in a food processor until smooth. Return mixture to the pan. Add orange juice and nutmeg. Stir over low heat until heated through. Spoon puree into centre of potato nest and serve.

PEAR AND SPINACH SALAD

Serves 6

- ☐ **1 bunch spinach, stalks removed and shredded**
- ☐ **2 spring onions, sliced**
- ☐ **3 slices ham, cut into thin strips**
- ☐ **2 pears, peeled, cored and diced**

DRESSING
- ☐ **2 tablespoons lemon juice**
- ☐ **1 tablespoon wholegrain mustard**
- ☐ **2 teaspoons sugar**
- ☐ **1 teaspoon dried tarragon leaves**
- ☐ **2 tablespoons olive oil**
- ☐ **1/2 cup (125 mL) vegetable oil**

1 Combine spinach, onions, ham and pears in a large glass serving dish. Toss gently. Pour over dressing and serve.

2 To make dressing, combine lemon juice, mustard, sugar, tarragon and oils in a screw top jar and shake until well mixed.

COOK'S TIP

If spring onions are not available, substitute shallots or white onions.

Plates Pillivuyt, Hale Imports *Tiles* Country Floors

Potato Nest with Carrot Puree and Pear and Spinach Salad

TOMATO AND CHEESE FRITTERS

These fritters are delicious served with choko pickles or your favourite chutney. Serve hot for a party snack, or as a tasty side dish at your next barbecue.

Serves 6

- ☐ **1/2 cup (80 g) bran**
- ☐ **1/2 cup (60 g) grated Swiss cheese**
- ☐ **2 tablespoons chopped fresh basil**
- ☐ **1/2 teaspoon caraway seeds**
- ☐ **3 medium, partially ripe tomatoes**
- ☐ **1/2 cup (60 g) plain flour, seasoned with freshly ground pepper**
- ☐ **2 eggs, beaten**
- ☐ **olive oil for cooking**

1 Combine bran, cheese, basil and caraway seeds. Cut tomatoes into 5 mm slices. Coat with seasoned flour, dip in egg, then coat with bran mixture.

2 Heat oil in a frypan. Cook tomato slices until golden brown. Drain on absorbent paper.

TIME SAVERS

■ Keep on hand a selection of cheeses to serve with wine and fruit. An easy entertaining idea for an impromptu get-together with friends. Don't forget to keep a good selection of crackers to accompany the cheese.

■ Read recipes through and assemble ingredients you need before starting.

■ Buy products that are partly prepared — cubed meat, grated cheese, instant lasagne and boned chicken. Many greengrocers and supermarkets also prepare fresh salads and vegetable mixes for soups and casseroles.

■ Look for new and interesting convenience products such as pasta sauces and casserole bases. There are many good quality brands available and some are also low in salt, low in fat and high in fibre.

Tomato and Cheese Fritters

Tiles Pazotti Tiles

HEALTHY LIFESTYLES

You'll be full of health and energy with these tempting, tasty recipes specially designed for today's active lifestyle.

HONEY GINGER VEGETABLES WITH WALNUTS

Serves 6

- ☐ **$^{3}/_{4}$ cup (190 mL) salad dressing**
- ☐ **1 teaspoon grated fresh ginger**
- ☐ **1 tablespoon honey**
- ☐ **2 tablespoons light soy sauce**
- ☐ **2 tablespoons lemon juice**
- ☐ **500 g thinly sliced butternut pumpkin**
- ☐ **250 g green beans, sliced**
- ☐ **3 zucchini, sliced**
- ☐ **$^{1}/_{2}$ cup (50 g) walnuts**

1 Heat dressing, ginger, honey, soy sauce and lemon juice in a frypan. Add pumpkin and cook until just tender.
2 Toss in combined beans and zucchini. Cook a further 3-4 minutes. Spoon onto a serving plate and serve topped with walnuts.

VEGETARIAN PIE

Serves 6

- ☐ **2 cups (300 g) cooked brown rice**
- ☐ **$1^{2}/_{3}$ cups (225 g) grated tasty cheese**
- ☐ **4 tablespoons grated Parmesan cheese**
- ☐ **2 shallots, chopped**
- ☐ **2 zucchini, grated**
- ☐ **1 carrot, peeled and grated**
- ☐ **1 cup (150 g) canned asparagus cuts, drained**
- ☐ **3 tablespoons pine nuts, toasted**
- ☐ **3 eggs, lightly beaten**
- ☐ **200 g unflavoured yoghurt**
- ☐ **freshly ground black pepper**

1 Combine rice, cheeses, shallots, zucchini, carrot, asparagus, pine nuts, eggs and yoghurt. Season with pepper.
2 Spoon mixture into a deep well-greased 23 cm springform pan. Bake at 190°C for 40 minutes or until firm. Cut into wedges to serve.

CAPSICUMS FILLED WITH HOT SPICY POTATO

A key ingredient in this recipe is the garam masala. Garam masala is a highly scented mix of cardamon seeds, cinnamon stick, nutmeg, mace and cumin seeds. Sometimes cloves and coriander are added for extra zest. It is readily available from supermarkets and delicatessens.

Serves 6

- ☐ **6 green or red capsicums**
- ☐ **60 g butter**
- ☐ **1 small red chilli, finely chopped**
- ☐ **1 onion, chopped**
- ☐ **4 potatoes, cooked, peeled and cubed**
- ☐ **$^{1}/_{2}$ teaspoon ground coriander**
- ☐ **$^{1}/_{4}$ teaspoon ground cumin powder**
- ☐ **$^{1}/_{2}$ teaspoon mustard seeds**
- ☐ **$^{1}/_{2}$ teaspoon turmeric**
- ☐ **$^{1}/_{2}$ teaspoon garam masala**
- ☐ **2 teaspoons lemon juice**

1 Cut a slice from the top of each capsicum. Remove seeds, keeping shells intact. Drop capsicums into a saucepan of boiling water and cook for 3 minutes. Drain and refresh under cold running water. Pat dry with absorbent paper.
2 Melt butter in a frypan. Add chilli, onion and potatoes, tossing over medium heat until golden brown. Stir in coriander, cumin, mustard seeds, turmeric and garam masala and cook for a further 1-2 minutes. Sprinkle over lemon juice.
3 Spoon potato mixture into capsicum shells. Place on a greased oven tray and bake at 180°C for 20 minutes.

Plates Villeroy & Boch Furniture Keyhole Furniture

Honey Ginger Vegetables with Walnuts, Vegetarian Pie and Capsicums Filled with Hot Spicy Potato

Cook's Tip

Use $^{3}/_{4}$ cup (140 g) raw brown rice to give 2 cups (300 g) cooked rice.

SAVOURY PUMPKIN FLAN

When incorporating beaten egg whites into a mixture, first stir one tablespoon of beaten egg white into mixture. Then, lightly fold remaining beaten egg white through, working as quickly as possible.

Serves 4

- ☐ **4 sheets filo pastry**
- ☐ **2 tablespoons polyunsaturated oil**
- ☐ **2 rashers bacon, chopped**
- ☐ **1 onion, chopped**
- ☐ **250 g pumpkin, peeled, cooked and mashed**
- ☐ **1 1/2 cups (180 g) grated tasty cheese**
- ☐ **2 eggs, separated**
- ☐ **2 tablespoons sour cream or unflavoured yoghurt**
- ☐ **freshly ground black pepper**
- ☐ **pinch chilli powder**
- ☐ **1 tablespoon chopped fresh parsley**

1 Brush each layer of pastry with oil and fold in half. Layer pastry, one folded piece on top of the other, to give eight layers. Place an 18 cm flan dish upside down on layered pastry and cut around dish making a circle 3 cm larger. Lift all layers of pastry into dish and roll down the edges.

2 Place bacon and onion in a frypan, and cook until bacon is crisp. Combine with pumpkin, cheese, egg yolks and sour cream. Season with pepper and chilli powder to taste.

3 Beat whites until stiff peaks form. Fold into pumpkin mixture and spoon into pastry case, sprinkle with parsley. Bake at 200°C for 30 minutes or until golden.

COOK'S TIP

As an alternative to salting food, use herbs and spices. But check labels carefully as some spicy mixes contain added salt.

Tray and Plate Barbara's House and Garden

Tuna and Tofu Sukiyaki and Crispy Salad with Honey Dressing

Savoury Pumpkin Flan

Plate Pillivuyt, Hale Imports

TUNA AND TOFU SUKIYAKI

Sukiyaki is traditionally cooked quickly in small batches so that the ingredients retain their moisture and crispness.

Serves 4

- ☐ **2 tablespoons polyunsaturated oil**
- ☐ **3 small onions, quartered**
- ☐ **6 small oyster mushrooms, sliced**
- ☐ **200 g bean sprouts**
- ☐ **5 spinach leaves, stalks removed, shredded**
- ☐ **1 red capsicum, sliced**
- ☐ **6 shallots, cut into 2.5 cm lengths**
- ☐ **250 g tofu, cubed**
- ☐ **440 g canned tuna, drained and flaked**
- ☐ **120 g transparent noodles, rinsed in cold water**
- ☐ **$^{1}/_{2}$ cup (125 mL) Japanese light soy sauce**
- ☐ **1 tablespoon sugar**

1 Heat 1 tablespoon of the oil in a frypan. Add half the onions, mushrooms, bean sprouts, spinach, capsicum, shallots, tofu, tuna and noodles to the pan.
2 Stir-fry quickly over high heat. Pour over half of the combined soy sauce and sugar. Serve immediately. Repeat with remaining ingredients.

CRISPY SALAD WITH HONEY DRESSING

Serves 6

- ☐ **2 carrots, cut into thin strips**
- ☐ **1 parsnip, cut into thin strips**
- ☐ **1 potato, cut into thin strips**
- ☐ **125 g green beans, sliced**
- ☐ **1 cooked beetroot, cut into thin strips**
- ☐ **1 red apple, chopped**
- ☐ **lemon juice**
- ☐ **1 tablespoon chopped fresh mint**

HONEY DRESSING

- ☐ **4 tablespoons Italian salad dressing**
- ☐ **4 tablespoons sour cream or unflavoured yoghurt**
- ☐ **1 tablespoon mayonnaise**
- ☐ **2 teaspoons honey**

1 Boil, steam or microwave carrots, parsnip, potato and beans until tender. Transfer to a serving plate. Top with beetroot, apple dipped in lemon juice and mint.
2 Combine salad dressing, sour cream, mayonnaise and honey in a saucepan. Heat gently, pour over salad and serve.

Plate Villa Italiana

Creamy Spinach in Zucchini and Cauliflower with Puffy Cheese Topping

CREAMY SPINACH IN ZUCCHINI

Fresh spinach may be used in place of frozen. Remove the stalks, shred the leaves and steam until soft.

Serves 6

- ☐ **6 medium zucchini**
- ☐ **250 g frozen spinach, thawed**
- ☐ **125 g ricotta cheese**
- ☐ **1/4 teaspoon ground nutmeg**
- ☐ **1 egg, beaten**
- ☐ **2 rashers bacon, chopped and cooked until crisp**
- ☐ **1/2 cup (60 g) grated tasty cheese**
- ☐ **paprika**

1 Trim ends from zucchini and drop into a saucepan of boiling water. Cook for 8-10 minutes or until just tender. Drain and halve lengthways. Carefully scoop out centres leaving shells with a little flesh. Finely chop scooped out flesh.

2 Squeeze spinach to remove liquid. Mix with chopped zucchini, ricotta, nutmeg and egg. Spoon into zucchini shells, top with combined bacon and cheese and dust lightly with paprika. Place on a greased oven tray and bake at 180°C for 15-20 minutes or until golden.

CAULIFLOWER WITH PUFFY CHEESE TOPPING

Serves 4

- ☐ **1/2 medium cauliflower, cut into florets**

SAUCE
- ☐ **30 g butter**
- ☐ **1 tablespoon plain flour**
- ☐ **1 cup (250 mL) milk**

HOT CHEESE TOPPING
- ☐ **2 egg whites**
- ☐ **2 tablespoons mayonnaise**
- ☐ **2 teaspoons sweet chilli sauce**
- ☐ **1/2 cup (60 g) grated tasty cheese**

1 Drop cauliflower florets in a saucepan of boiling water and cook for 8-10 minutes or until tender. Drain and transfer to a greased ovenproof dish.

2 To make sauce, melt butter in a saucepan, add flour, cook for 1 minute. Blend in milk, stirring over heat until sauce boils and thickens. Pour sauce over cauliflower.

3 To make topping, beat egg whites until stiff peaks form. Fold through combined mayonnaise and chilli sauce. Spoon over cauliflower mixture. Top with cheese. Bake at 220°C for 10-15 minutes or until puffed and golden.

COOK'S TIP

If your sauce has turned lumpy remove it from the heat and beat briskly with a wire balloon whisk or process in a food processor until smooth. Add more liquid if too thick and reheat.

SPICY NUT MEATBALLS

You can purchase canned nut meat and vegetable protein in most retail health food outlets. Vegetable protein is in a dehydrated form and is reconstituted when liquid is added.

Serves 4

- ☐ **2 carrots, peeled and sliced**
- ☐ **1 parsnip, peeled and sliced**
- ☐ **3 teaspoons vegetable extract blended with 2 cups (500 mL) water**
- ☐ **1 tablespoon cornflour blended with 3 tablespoons water**
- ☐ **430 g canned nut meat**
- ☐ **2 teaspoons (TVP) vegetable protein**
- ☐ **$^1/_4$ teaspoon dried thyme**
- ☐ **$^1/_2$ teaspoon dried rosemary**
- ☐ **1 clove garlic, crushed**
- ☐ **seasoned plain flour**
- ☐ **1 tablespoon polyunsaturated oil**
- ☐ **4 shallots, cut into 2.5 cm lengths**

1 Place carrots and parsnip in a saucepan, pour over blended vegetable extract. Cover and cook for 10-12 minutes or until tender.

2 Whisk blended cornflour into pan. Stir over heat until mixture boils and thickens.

3 Mash nut meat and stir in vegetable protein, thyme, rosemary and garlic. Shape into small balls and toss in seasoned flour. Heat oil in frypan, cook nut meat balls until well browned. Drain and arrange on a serving dish.

4 Toss shallots in pan, cooking for 1-2 minutes. Sprinkle over nut meat balls. Spoon vegetables over and serve.

TWO PEA SALAD

Serves 4

- ☐ **500 g frozen peas**
- ☐ **150 g snow peas, trimmed**
- ☐ **1 clove garlic, crushed**
- ☐ **2 tablespoons polyunsaturated oil**
- ☐ **2 teaspoons lemon juice**
- ☐ **1 small onion, thinly sliced**

1 Drop frozen peas into a saucepan of boiling water. Cook for 3-4 minutes. Add snow peas for the last minute of cooking. Drain.

2 Spoon peas into a glass salad bowl and season to taste. Toss in combined garlic, oil and lemon juice. Cool to room temperature. Fold through sliced onion.

Spicy Nut Meatballs and Two Pea Salad

Plates Villa Italiana

Plate Villeroy & Boch *Tiles* Pazotti Tiles

Cheesy Mushroom Slice

STEP-BY-STEP

CHEESY MUSHROOM SLICE

This recipe is an ideal one to cook ahead. Prepare the whole dish, cover and refrigerate overnight. Bake when you are ready the next day. The flavour develops if allowed to stand before cooking.

Serves 6

- ☐ **60 g butter**
- ☐ **3 rashers bacon, chopped**
- ☐ **400 g mushrooms, sliced**
- ☐ **4 shallots, chopped**
- ☐ **1 small green capsicum, chopped**
- ☐ **1 small red capsicum, chopped**
- ☐ **6 thick slices white bread, crusts removed**
- ☐ **1 cup (125 g) grated tasty cheese**
- ☐ **6 eggs**
- ☐ **2 cups (500 mL) milk**
- ☐ **1 tablespoon mayonnaise**
- ☐ **1 teaspoon French mustard**
- ☐ **1 teaspoon Worcestershire sauce**
- ☐ **2 tablespoons chopped fresh parsley**

1 Melt butter in a frypan. Cook bacon until crisp, stir in mushrooms, shallots and capsicums, cook until mushrooms are soft.

2 Cut bread slices into 2.5 cm pieces. Place half the bread in a single layer in a greased 28 cm x 17 cm ovenproof dish. Spoon over mushroom mixture and top with remaining bread. Sprinkle over cheese.

3 Whisk together eggs, milk, mayonnaise, mustard and Worcestershire sauce. Pour over bread mixture, sprinkle top with parsley and bake at 180°C for 50-60 minutes.

Cut bread into 2.5 cm pieces

Spoon mushroom mixture over bread in base of dish

Pour egg, milk, mayonnaise, mustard and sauce over bread mixture

Cook's Tip

Always use vegetables that are as fresh as possible. They should be well washed before cooking but not soaked. Remembering these two facts will ensure that you get the maximum nutritional value from your vegetables.

Plate Villa Italiana *Tiles* Country Floors

PICKLED TOMATOES AND BEANS

This recipe uses canned three bean mix which is made up of a mixture of butter beans, kidney beans and lima beans. Any canned mixed beans can be used as a substitute.

Serves 4

- ☐ **2 tablespoons olive oil**
- ☐ **1 clove garlic, crushed**
- ☐ **1 tablespoon chopped fresh basil**

Carrot Balls

Plates Mid City Home and Garden *Tiles* Country Floors

CARROT BALLS

Serves 4

- ☐ **3 carrots, peeled and grated**
- ☐ **2 teaspoons orange rind**
- ☐ **$^1/_2$ cup (60 g) grated Swiss cheese**
- ☐ **$^1/_2$ cup (60 g) grated Parmesan cheese**
- ☐ **1 tablespoon chopped fresh mint**
- ☐ **2 eggs, lightly beaten**
- ☐ **plain flour**
- ☐ **1 cup (190 g) bran**
- ☐ **3 tablespoons finely chopped almonds**
- ☐ **polyunsaturated oil for cooking**

1 Combine carrots, orange rind, cheeses, mint and half the egg mixture. Season to taste. Shape into balls. Coat with flour, dip in remaining beaten egg and roll in combined bran and almonds.

2 Heat oil in a frypan. Cook carrot balls until golden brown. Drain on absorbent paper. Serve with mango chutney if desired.

Nutrition Tip

An alternative low fat cooking method is to lightly oil a baking dish and place the carrot balls in it. Bake the carrot balls on 200°C for 15-20 minutes, turning frequently during the cooking time for a delicious, crusty texture.

- ☐ **310 g canned three bean mix, drained**
- ☐ **250 g cherry tomatoes, halved**
- ☐ **$2^1/_2$ teaspoons white vinegar**
- ☐ **$^1/_2$ teaspoon sugar**

1 Heat oil in a frypan. Cook garlic and basil for 1 minute, stir in beans and tomatoes. Season to taste.

2 Cover and simmer for 5-6 minutes. Mix in combined vinegar and sugar. Heat through gently and serve.

Pickled Tomatoes and Beans and Potatoes Filled with Chilli Beans

POTATOES FILLED WITH CHILLI BEANS

You can substitute butter beans or a three bean mix for kidney beans.

Serves 4

- ☐ **4 medium potatoes**
- ☐ **310 g canned red kidney beans**
- ☐ **1 tablespoon tomato paste**
- ☐ **1-2 teaspoons chilli sauce (according to taste)**
- ☐ **paprika**

1 Bake scrubbed, unpeeled potatoes at 220°C for 45 minutes-1hour or until soft but firm. Cool slightly.

2 Cut potatoes in half and scoop out flesh, leaving a thin shell. Mash potato flesh and combine with beans, tomato paste and sauce.

3 Spoon mixture back into potato shells. Dust lightly with paprika and bake at 200°C until heated through and lightly browned on top.

MICROWAVE IT

Potatoes can also be microwaved on HIGH (100%) for 4-5 minutes. Stand for 5 minutes before removing flesh.

CHICKEN AND MUSHROOM STRUDEL

This recipe is also delicious made with tuna or salmon in place of the chicken. Ricotta cheese can be substituted for cream cheese.

Serves 6

- ☐ **10 sheets filo pastry**
- ☐ **4 tablespoons polyunsaturated oil**

FILLING

- ☐ **200 g soft cream cheese**
- ☐ **2 cooked chicken fillets, cut into thin strips**
- ☐ **1/2 red capsicum, sliced**
- ☐ **8 small mushrooms, sliced**
- ☐ **1 avocado, peeled, stoned and sliced**
- ☐ **2 teaspoons curry powder**
- ☐ **dried onion flakes to taste**
- ☐ **2 tablespoons sesame seeds**

1 Layer filo pastry sheets on top of each other, brushing between layers with oil.

2 To make filling, spread cream cheese down the long edge of pastry, leaving approximately 5 cm at each end. Top with chicken, capsicum, mushrooms and avocado. Sprinkle with curry powder and onion flakes.

3 Roll up tightly, tucking ends under and place on an oven tray. Brush top with oil and sprinkle with sesame seeds. Bake at 180°C for 30 minutes or until lightly browned.

Chicken and Mushroom Strudel

Plates Mid City Home and Garden

BRUSSELS SPROUTS AND ALMONDS IN TANGY SAUCE

Serves 4

- ☐ **500 g brussels sprouts**
- ☐ **3 tablespoons toasted almond flakes**

TANGY SAUCE

- ☐ **30 g butter, melted**
- ☐ **2 tablespoons brown sugar**
- ☐ **3 teaspoons cornflour**
- ☐ **1/2 teaspoon prepared mustard**
- ☐ **1 small onion, finely chopped**
- ☐ **3 tablespoons white vinegar**

1 Boil, steam or microwave brussels sprouts until tender. Drain and keep warm.

2 Combine butter, sugar, cornflour, mustard, onion and vinegar in a saucepan. Cook, stirring until sauce boils and thickens. Pour over brussels sprouts, with toasted almonds and serve.

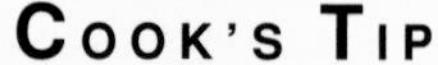

When steaming vegetables of different textures together, place the vegetable that will take longer to cook on the bottom of the steamer where it will cook more rapidly.

MOULDED TOMATO RISOTTO

Serves 6

- ☐ **3 tablespoons olive oil**
- ☐ **2 onions, chopped**
- ☐ **500 g quick-cook brown rice**
- ☐ **440 g canned tomatoes**
- ☐ **3 tablespoons tomato paste**
- ☐ **1 litre chicken stock**
- ☐ **90 g butter**
- ☐ **100 g Parmesan cheese, grated**
- ☐ **freshly ground black pepper**
- ☐ **2 tablespoons chopped fresh basil**
- ☐ **zucchini ribbons for garnish**

Plates Villa Italiana

Brussels Sprouts and Almonds in Tangy Sauce

1 Heat oil in a frypan, cook onions until golden, add rice, tossing to coat grains. Pour in combined mashed, undrained tomatoes, tomato paste and boiling stock. Stir over heat until rice is cooked and all of the liquid has been absorbed.

2 Fold through butter, Parmesan, pepper to taste and basil. Spoon into a well-greased ovenproof bowl. Cover and bake at 200°C for 10-15 minutes. Turn out onto a serving plate and decorate top with zucchini ribbons.

Cook's Tip

To make zucchini ribbons, cut long thin slices from top to base of zucchini using a vegetable peeler.

Plate Mid City Home and Garden

Moulded Tomato Risotto

Sweet REWARDS

Extravagant ways with fruit, wicked use of cream, pies that melt in the mouth and classic favourites will tempt even the most determined to a sweet reward.

CHOCOLATE ORANGE PUMPKIN PIE

Serves 8

CRUMB CRUST

- ☐ **125 g sweet un-iced chocolate biscuits, crushed**
- ☐ **3 tablespoons finely chopped walnuts**
- ☐ **90 g butter, melted**

FILLING

- ☐ **250 g pumpkin, peeled and cooked**
- ☐ **2 teaspoons grated orange rind**
- ☐ **$\frac{3}{4}$ cup (190 mL) cream**
- ☐ **2 eggs, separated**
- ☐ **1 teaspoon mixed spice**
- ☐ **$\frac{1}{4}$ teaspoon ground nutmeg**
- ☐ **$\frac{2}{3}$ cup (120 g) brown sugar**
- ☐ **$1\frac{1}{2}$ tablespoons gelatine dissolved in 3 tablespoons hot water**

1 To make crust, combine crushed biscuits and walnuts in a bowl. Stir in melted butter. Press mixture over base and sides of a 20 cm pie plate. Refrigerate.

2 To make filling, puree pumpkin, orange rind, 3 tablespoons cream, egg yolks, spice, nutmeg and sugar in a blender or food processor. Pour mixture into a saucepan and stir over medium heat until hot but not boiling. Whisk dissolved gelatine into pumpkin mixture. Allow to cool and refrigerate until almost set. Check every 15 minutes.

3 Whip extra cream and fold through filling with beaten egg whites. Spoon into biscuit base and refrigerate until set. Decorate top with cream and chocolate curls if desired.

Cook's Tip

Gelatine can be a little tricky if not used correctly. The dissolved gelatine and the food must be at similar temperatures before combining.

APPLE AND BERRY PLAIT

Serves 4

- ☐ **24 sheets filo pastry**
- ☐ **125 g butter, melted**
- ☐ **icing sugar**

APPLE FILLING

- ☐ **410 g canned pie apple**
- ☐ **1 teaspoon grated lemon rind**
- ☐ **3 tablespoons sultanas**
- ☐ **1 tablespoon honey**

BERRY FILLING

- ☐ **$1\frac{1}{2}$ cups (400 g) canned blueberries, drained**
- ☐ **3 tablespoons ground almonds**

1 Layer eight filo pastry sheets on top of each other. Brush between each sheet with butter. Repeat with remaining pastry.

2 To make apple filling, combine apple, lemon rind, sultanas and honey. Spoon half the mixture down the long edge of one pastry layer, leaving 5 cm at each end and roll up tightly. Repeat with remaining apple mixture and another pastry layer.

3 To make berry filling, combine blueberries and almonds. Spoon down remaining pastry layer as above. Place rolls side by side on an oven tray, then form into a plait, tucking ends under. Brush with butter and bake at 200°C for 40-45 minutes until golden. Cool slightly and dust with icing sugar before serving.

Watchpoint

When working with filo pastry, cover any sheets that are not immediately in use with a dampened tea towel, to prevent drying.

Plate Mid City Home and Garden

Chocolate Orange Pumpkin Pie, Apple and Berry Plait and Almond Biscuit Baskets (see page 42)

ALMOND BISCUIT BASKETS

Any filling such as fresh berries can be used with this delicious recipe. If the filling is liquid, fill and serve immediately to prevent biscuit softening.

Serves 4

- ☐ **1 egg white**
- ☐ **4 tablespoons icing sugar**
- ☐ **$^1/_2$ teaspoon vanilla**
- ☐ **30 g butter**
- ☐ **30 g ground almonds**
- ☐ **3 tablespoons plain flour**
- ☐ **vanilla ice cream**
- ☐ **caramel topping**
- ☐ **4 tablespoons chopped almonds**

1 Beat egg white with a fork until foamy. Gradually stir in sifted icing sugar, vanilla, melted butter and almonds. Fold in sifted flour.

2 Lightly grease two oven trays. Mark two 16 cm circles on each tray, using a saucer as a guide. Drop spoonfuls of mixture into circles, spread to fill circles. Bake at 220°C for 5-6 minutes or until biscuits are light golden brown around edges.

3 Lift biscuits quickly from trays. Carefully place biscuit in one hand and using a small glass or jar, shape biscuit around and hold in place until biscuit is firm, this will take about 1 minute. When cool, place a scoop of ice cream into each basket, pour over caramel topping and sprinkle with chopped almonds.

BANANA FLAMBE WITH HONEY AVOCADO SAUCE

Serves 4

- ☐ **60 g unsalted butter**
- ☐ **2$^1/_2$ tablespoons brown sugar**
- ☐ **4 bananas, peeled, halved lengthways**
- ☐ **1 tablespoon lemon juice**
- ☐ **4 tablespoons rum**

AVOCADO AND HONEY SAUCE

- ☐ **1 avocado, peeled, stoned and chopped**
- ☐ **1 tablespoon honey**
- ☐ **1 tablespoon lemon juice**
- ☐ **150 mL cream**

1 Melt butter in a frypan. Add sugar and stir over heat until sugar dissolves. Toss in bananas and lemon juice. Cook for 1-2 minutes each side. Pour over rum. Heat for a few seconds then light. Shake pan until flames die.

2 To make sauce, combine avocado, honey, lemon juice and cream in the bowl of a food processor. Process until smooth. Place bananas on a serving plate, spoon over sauce and serve.

NUTRITION TIP

Evaporated skim milk makes a good substitute for thin cream. It also whips like cream if kept chilled.

Cream Cheese Crepes with Cherry Sauce

Banana Flambe with Honey Avocado Sauce and Snowballs

Plate Villeroy & Boch *Tiles* Pazotti Tiles

COOK'S TIP

Packaged dried shredded coconut is available in most supermarkets and health food outlets.

Plate Mid City Home and Garden

SNOWBALLS

Serves 4

- ☐ **4 ripe pears, peeled, stalks left intact**
- ☐ **2 egg whites**
- ☐ **4 tablespoons caster sugar**
- ☐ **1 cup (90 g) shredded coconut**
- ☐ **30 g flaked almonds**

1 Stand pears in a large saucepan with water to a depth of 1 cm. Cover and simmer for 8-10 minutes or until just tender. Cool.

2 Beat egg whites until soft peaks form. Add sugar a spoonful at a time, beating well after each addition. Continue to beat until mixture is thick and glossy.

3 Cover pears with meringue. Chop coconut roughly and sprinkle over pears. Top with almonds. Place on a greased oven tray. Bake at 180°C for 5 minutes or until meringue is lightly browned.

CREAM CHEESE CREPES WITH CHERRY SAUCE

Serves 6

- ☐ **250 g cream cheese**
- ☐ **2 tablespoons Kirsch**
- ☐ **2 tablespoons caster sugar**
- ☐ **1/2 teaspoon vanilla essence**
- ☐ **425 g canned pitted black cherries, drained and liquid reserved**
- ☐ **6 prepared crepes**
- ☐ **2 teaspoons cornflour blended with 3 tablespoons water**

1 Combine cream cheese, Kirsch, sugar and vanilla in a mixing bowl. Beat until smooth and gently fold in cherries. Spoon cheese mixture onto crepes, fold in sides and roll up. Arrange crepes in well-greased ovenproof dish. Bake at 180°C for 10 minutes.

2 Place reserved cherry liquid into a saucepan. Bring to the boil, reduce heat and whisk in blended cornflour, stir until sauce thickens. Arrange crepes on serving plates, spoon over sauce and serve.

COOK'S TIP

Prepared crepes are available in some supermarkets, however you can easily make them yourself. The following recipe will make 10 crepes. Crepes freeze very well so can be made in advance to have on hand when needed. Place cooked crepes between sheets of greaseproof paper and pack into freezer bags.

- ☐ **3/4 cup (185 g) plain flour, sifted**
- ☐ **1/2 cup (125mL) water**
- ☐ **1/2 cup (125mL) milk**
- ☐ **2 eggs**
- ☐ **butter for cooking**

Combine flour, water, milk and eggs in a large bowl. Mix until smooth. Melt a little butter in a crepe pan and pour in 2 tablespoons mixture. Cook for 1 minute each side until pale golden.

STEP-BY-STEP

BRANDY GRAPE FLAN

Serves 8

- ☐ **1 sheet prepared shortcrust pastry, thawed**

FILLING
- ☐ **250 g cream cheese**
- ☐ **2 tablespoons bottled lemon butter**
- ☐ **1 tablespoon icing sugar**
- ☐ **500 g large green grapes**

GLAZE
- ☐ **3 tablespoons apricot jam**
- ☐ **$1^1/_2$ tablespoons water**
- ☐ **2 teaspoons brandy**

1 Line a lightly greased 20 cm flan tin with pastry. Trim edge and bake blind at 200°C for 10 minutes. Remove rice and paper. Reduce temperature to 180°C and bake a further 15-20 minutes or until pastry is light golden. Cool.

2 To make filling, beat cream cheese until soft. Mix in lemon butter and icing sugar. Spread cream cheese mixture over the base of cooled pastry case.

3 Wash grapes and separate from stems. Cut in half and remove seeds. Arrange grapes in a decorative pattern over cream cheese mixture.

4 To make glaze, heat apricot jam and water in a saucepan, stirring until jam melts. Push through a sieve. Stir in brandy and cool slightly. Brush over grapes.

Cook's Tip

To bake blind, cover pastry with baking paper and weight with uncooked rice or pasta. Cook for 10 minutes at 200°C. Remove rice and paper, reduce temperature to 180°C and bake 15-20 minutes until pastry is a light golden colour.

Line a 20 cm flan tin

Arrange grapes in a decorative pattern over cream cheese mixture

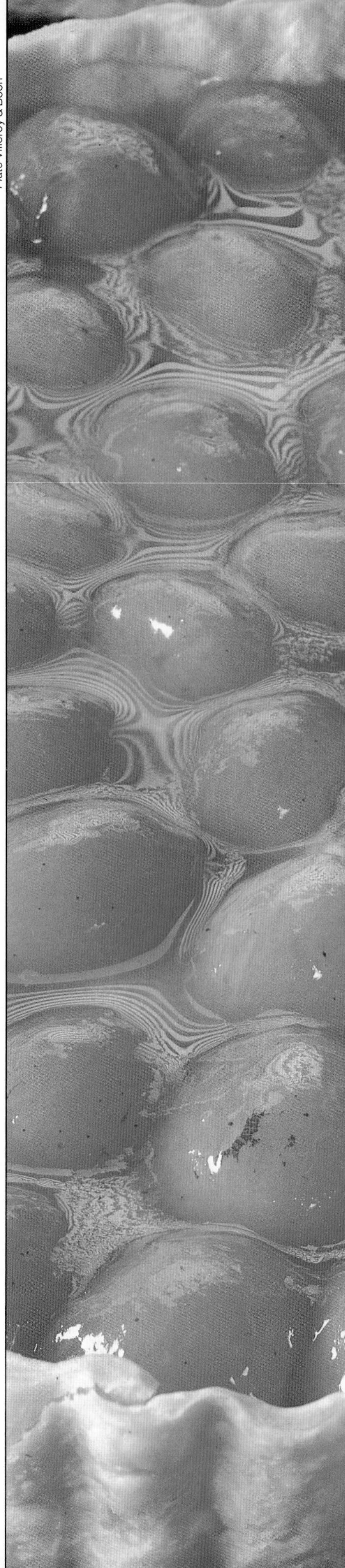

Brandy Grape Flan

Plate Villeroy & Boch

Brush glaze over grapes

GINGER MELON SALAD

Serves 6

- ☐ **3 melons, each about 500 g (e.g. rockmelon, honeydew, watermelon)**
- ☐ **2 tablespoons caster sugar**
- ☐ **2 tablespoons Grand Marnier**
- ☐ **4 pieces preserved ginger**

1 Halve melons and remove seeds. Scoop out flesh with a melon baller. Place balls in a glass serving dish.

2 Sprinkle over caster sugar and Grand Marnier. Toss lightly. Garnish with finely chopped ginger and chill before serving.

TIME SAVER

Save time by storing melons in the refrigerator when you buy them. You will then be able to serve your chilled melon salad immediately.

Ginger Melon Salad

Bowls Barbara's House and Garden

Plates Villeroy & Boch

LEMON AND LIME MERINGUE PIE

This delicious pie can be made up and frozen until required. Thaw in the refrigerator for a few hours, then bake at 150°C for 20-25 minutes.

Serves 8

- ☐ **180 g plain sweet biscuits**
- ☐ **1 teaspoon cinnamon**
- ☐ **125 g butter, melted**
- ☐ **400 g canned sweetened condensed milk**
- ☐ **3 tablespoons lemon juice**
- ☐ **3 tablespoons lime juice**
- ☐ **2 teaspoons grated lemon rind**
- ☐ **2 teaspoons lime rind**
- ☐ **2 egg yolks**
- ☐ **4 egg whites**
- ☐ **3 tablespoons sugar**

1 Crush biscuits in a food processor to make fine crumbs. Combine crumbs, cinnamon and melted butter. Press over base and sides of a 23 cm pie dish and refrigerate.

2 Combine condensed milk, juices, rind and egg yolks. Spoon into crumb crust.

3 Beat egg whites well, adding sugar and beating until stiff and glossy. Spoon over filling and bake at 180°C for 10-12 minutes or until golden.

PEARS WITH MACAROON FILLING

You can make this recipe with canned peach halves if you prefer.

Serves 6

- ☐ **6 canned pear halves, drained**
- ☐ **$^{3}/_{4}$ cup (90 g) crushed macaroon biscuits**
- ☐ **1 egg yolk, beaten**
- ☐ **2 tablespoons caster sugar**
- ☐ **45 g butter, softened**

1 Scoop a little of the flesh from pear halves to make a deeper cavity. Add chopped flesh to crushed macaroons in a heatproof bowl. Stir in egg yolk, sugar and butter. Stir over a saucepan of simmering water until blended. Cool.

2 Spoon mixture into pear halves. Arrange in greased ovenproof dish and bake at 180°C for 25-30 minutes or until golden. Serve with cream or ice cream if desired.

Lemon and Lime Meringue Pie and Pears with Macaroon Filling

Cook's Tip

To prepare souffle dish, grease lightly with melted butter and coat base and sides with caster sugar.

Plate Villeroy & Boch *Tiles* Pazotti Tiles

SIMPLE SOUFFLE

If you do not have any stale cake crumbs, increase the amount of sponge fingers to make up the difference.

Serves 4

- ☐ **30 g butter**
- ☐ **2 tablespoons plain flour**
- ☐ **$1^1/_2$ cups (375mL) milk**
- ☐ **4 sponge fingers, crushed**
- ☐ **$^3/_4$ cup (100 g) stale cake crumbs**
- ☐ **4 egg yolks**
- ☐ **5 egg whites**

1 Melt butter in saucepan and stir in flour, cook for 1 minute. Blend in milk, stirring until sauce boils and thickens. Remove from heat and stir in crushed sponge fingers, cake crumbs and egg yolks.

2 Beat egg whites until stiff peaks form. Fold into cake mixture and spoon into prepared 18 cm souffle dish. Bake at 200°C for 20 minutes. Serve with whipped cream if desired.

CHILLED PEACH CREAM

Serves 6

- ☐ **850 g canned peaches in syrup**
- ☐ **3 teaspoons gelatine**
- ☐ **1 cup (250 mL) cream, whipped**

1 Drain peaches, reserving syrup. Puree peaches in a food processor. Measure puree to make $1^1/_4$ cups (310 mL). Reserve remaining puree.

2 Sprinkle gelatine over 3 tablespoons reserved syrup and dissolve over hot water. Cool and whisk into peach puree. Fold in whipped cream.

3 Pour mixture into a rinsed fluted mould or six individual moulds. Chill until set. Turn out and serve with remaining puree and cream if desired.

Microwave It

Dissolve the gelatine in syrup in the microwave. Cook on HIGH (100%) for 40 seconds.

Simple Souffle,
Chilled Peach Cream and
Lemon and Passionfruit Cream

LEMON AND PASSIONFRUIT CREAM

Pineapple jelly crystals and 1/2 cup (125 mL) crushed pineapple can be used in place of lemon jelly and passionfruit.

Serves 4

- ☐ **100 g packet lemon jelly crystals**
- ☐ **1/2 cup (125 mL) hot water**
- ☐ **1/2 cup (125 mL) cold water**
- ☐ **1 cup (250 mL) evaporated milk, chilled**
- ☐ **pulp 9 passionfruit**
- ☐ **1/2 cup (125 mL) cream, whipped**

1 Place jelly crystals and hot water in a bowl. Stir until crystals dissolve and pour in cold water.

2 Beat evaporated milk in a bowl until thick. Stir in jelly mixture and 1/2 cup (125 mL) passionfruit pulp. Spoon into six individual glass serving dishes and refrigerate until firm. Decorate top with whipped cream and remaining passionfruit pulp.

CHESTNUT LOG

Serves 8

- ☐ **440 g canned sweetened chestnut puree**
- ☐ **125 g unsalted butter, softened**
- ☐ **1 egg**
- ☐ **2-3 drops vanilla essence**
- ☐ **3 tablespoons rum**
- ☐ **24 sponge fingers**

GLAZE

- ☐ **2 tablespoons cocoa**
- ☐ **1 tablespoon caster sugar**
- ☐ **2 tablespoons water**

ICING

- ☐ **3/4 cup (125 g) icing sugar**
- ☐ **125 g unsalted butter, softened**
- ☐ **1 tablespoon coffee essence**

1 Combine chestnut puree, butter, egg, vanilla, half the rum in a mixing bowl and beat until smooth. Grease and line the base and sides of a 9 cm x 22 cm loaf pan with sponge fingers and sprinkle with remaining rum. Spoon in chestnut mixture and top with sponge fingers. Refrigerate until firm.

2 Turn log out onto a serving plate.

3 To make glaze, combine cocoa, sugar and water in a heatproof bowl. Stir over simmering water, until sugar has dissolved and glaze is smooth. Cool and brush three-quarters of the glaze over chilled log.

4 To make icing, cream together icing sugar, butter and coffee essence. Beat until well blended. Decorate log with piped rosettes of icing and drizzle over remaining glaze. Serve sliced with cream or ice-cream if desired.

COOK'S TIP

If coffee essence is unavailable, substitute 1 teaspoon of instant coffee dissolved in 1 tablespoon hot water.

Chestnut Log

Eat In Or TAKE AWAY

Indulge in these tasty barbecue and picnic ideas which won't keep you long in the kitchen when you are planning to eat al fresco.

BARBECUED LEG OF LAMB WITH LEMON HERB BUTTER

Serves 8

- ☐ **1 boned leg of lamb**
- ☐ **2 cloves garlic, cut into slivers**
- ☐ **2 sprigs fresh rosemary**
- ☐ **freshly ground black pepper**

LEMON HERB BUTTER
- ☐ **125 g butter, softened**
- ☐ **2 teaspoons grated lemon rind**
- ☐ **1 tablespoon chopped fresh basil**
- ☐ **1 tablespoon chopped fresh parsley**
- ☐ **1 tablespoon lemon juice**
- ☐ **1 teaspoon sweet chilli sauce**

1 Trim meat of excess fat. Make three deep slashes on top of meat with a sharp knife and tuck slivers of garlic and rosemary leaves into each.Sprinkle liberally with pepper.
2 To make Lemon Herb Butter, combine butter, rind, basil, parsley, lemon juice and sauce and mix well.
3 Barbecue or grill lamb over gentle heat, basting with lemon herb butter until tender.

POTATO SALAD AND AVOCADO DRESSING

Serves 6

- ☐ **1 kg tiny new potatoes, scrubbed**
- ☐ **2 tablespoons chopped fresh parsley**
- ☐ **6 hardboiled eggs, quartered**
- ☐ **1 onion, sliced**

AVOCADO DRESSING
- ☐ **1 avocado, peeled and stoned**
- ☐ **1 clove garlic, crushed**
- ☐ **1 tablespoon lemon juice**
- ☐ **$^1/_2$ cup (125 g) light sour cream**
- ☐ **2 drops Tabasco sauce**
- ☐ **1 teaspoon honey**

1 Boil or steam potatoes until tender. Drain and place potatoes in a salad bowl with parsley, eggs and onion.
2 To make dressing, process avocado, garlic, lemon juice, sour cream, sauce and honey in a food processor or blender until smooth.

Nutrition Tip

Try low-fat unflavoured yoghurt in recipes instead of sour cream. If using in hot food, stir through at the end of cooking and do not allow to boil or it will go grainy.

GLAZED FRUIT KEBABS

Serves 4

- ☐ **225 g canned pineapple pieces**
- ☐ **1 cooking apple, peeled and cubed**
- ☐ **2 large bananas, thickly sliced**
- ☐ **250 g strawberries, washed and hulled**
- ☐ **2 kiwi fruit, peeled and cubed**
- ☐ **1 orange, segmented**

GLAZE
- ☐ **$^1/_2$ cup (125mL) orange juice**
- ☐ **1 tablespoon honey**
- ☐ **1 tablespoon Grand Marnier**
- ☐ **2 teaspoons cornflour**

1 Thread fruit pieces onto eight oiled wooden skewers, alternating the pieces attractively.
2 To make glaze, combine ingredients in a saucepan. Cook over medium heat 2-3 minutes until glaze boils and thickens.
3 Barbecue or grill over gentle heat, turning and brushing frequently with glaze.

Plates Villa Italiana, Mosman

Barbecued Leg of Lamb with Lemon Herb Butter, Potato Salad and Avocado Dressing and Glazed Fruit Kebabs

Cook's Tip

When using wooden skewers, don't forget to soak them in cold water for at least an hour before using under grill or over a barbecue, as they can burn.

Dish Mid City Home and Garden

Layered Pork and Chicken Loaf

LAYERED PORK AND CHICKEN LOAF

Serves 6

- ☐ **30 g butter**
- ☐ **1 onion, chopped**
- ☐ **1 clove garlic, crushed**
- ☐ **2 pork fillets, minced**
- ☐ **3 tablespoons chopped fresh parsley**
- ☐ **2 eggs**
- ☐ **2 teaspoons canned green peppercorns**
- ☐ **1 tablespoon dry vermouth**
- ☐ **500 g roll prepared puff pastry, thawed**
- ☐ **2 chicken fillets, lightly pounded**
- ☐ **1 egg white**

1 Melt butter in a frypan, cook onion and garlic for 2-3 minutes until golden. Combine with minced pork, parsley, eggs, peppercorns and vermouth.

2 Open out puff pastry roll and cut off a 40 cm length. Cut an 8 cm square from each corner. This eliminates bulkiness when folded. Press pork mixture down centre of pastry to form rectangle shape. Top with chicken fillets. Wrap up like a parcel and decorate top with leaves cut from pastry scraps.

3 Brush with beaten egg white and place on a greased roasting rack in a baking dish. Bake at 180°C for 1-1$^{1}/_{4}$ hours or until pastry is golden and crisp. Serve hot or cold accompanied with mango chutney or tomato relish.

COOK'S TIP

If any recipe calls for 'prepared pastry', use your own favourite recipe or the quicker, more convenient ready-rolled pastry. As this is usually frozen, it is important to remember to thaw it before starting the recipe. Thawed pastry blocks can also be used.

GREEN FRUIT SALAD

If Creme de Menthe is unavailable, substitute sweet sherry or lemon juice.

Serves 6

- ☐ **500 g green grapes**
- ☐ **1 Granny Smith apple**
- ☐ **4 kiwi fruit**
- ☐ **1 honeydew melon**
- ☐ **1 tablespoon chopped fresh mint**

SYRUP

- ☐ **$^{1}/_{2}$ cup (125 g) sugar**
- ☐ **$^{3}/_{4}$ cup (190 mL) water**
- ☐ **1$^{1}/_{2}$ tablespoons Creme de Menthe Liqueur**
- ☐ **1 strip lemon peel**

1 Wash grapes and separate from stems. Wash, core and slice apple. Peel and chop kiwi fruit. Halve melon, remove seeds and scoop out flesh with a melon baller. Arrange fruit in a bowl.

2 To make syrup, combine sugar, water, liqueur and lemon peel in a saucepan, stir over heat until sugar has dissolved. Bring to the boil, reduce heat and simmer for 7 minutes. Allow to cool.
3 Pour cooled syrup over fruit and chill until serving time.

SRI LANKAN PRAWN SALAD

Serves 6

- ☐ **1 kg cooked king prawns, peeled and deveined**
- ☐ **1 grapefruit, segmented**
- ☐ **1 orange, segmented**
- ☐ **2 bananas, peeled and sliced**
- ☐ **1 onion, sliced**
- ☐ **6 spinach leaves, shredded**
- ☐ **1/2 cup (60 g) chopped cashew nuts**

DRESSING

- ☐ **2 tablespoons lemon juice**
- ☐ **250 g unflavoured yoghurt**
- ☐ **1 teaspoon curry powder**
- ☐ **2 tablespoons mayonnaise**

1 Combine prawns, fruit, onion and spinach in a salad bowl. Pour dressing over salad and toss gently. Sprinkle over cashew nuts. Cover and chill.
2 To make dressing, combine juice, yoghurt, curry powder and mayonnaise.

TIME SAVER

For quick and easy salads, save time by storing ingredients (and even some canned products) in the refrigerator. Salads can then be served immediately.

BACON AND BANANA KEBABS

Serves 6

- ☐ **6 rashers bacon**
- ☐ **6 firm bananas**
- ☐ **3 small onions, quartered**
- ☐ **1 red capsicum, cubed**
- ☐ **1 tablespoon oil**

1 Remove rind from bacon and cut each rasher into four. Peel bananas and cut each into four.
2 Wrap a piece of bacon around each piece of banana and thread onto six oiled wooden skewers alternating with onion and capsicum. Brush with oil and barbecue or grill until bacon is crisp.

Green Fruit Salad, Sri Lankan Prawn Salad and Bacon and Banana Kebabs

COOK'S TIP

When barbecuing always have a bottle of water with a sprinkle top on hand so that you can douse any flames that are caused by fat dripping on to the coals.

Plate Villeroy & Boch

Remove bones from snapper

Segment orange for stuffing

Cook's Tip

Snapper is a warm water sea fish with a delicate white flesh — if unavailable substitute sea bream or any other white-fleshed fish.

Whole Fish with Orange and Tomato Butter

STEP-BY-STEP

WHOLE FISH WITH ORANGE AND TOMATO BUTTER

Serves 2

- ☐ **1 kg whole snapper**
- ☐ **30 g butter**
- ☐ **3 shallots, finely chopped**
- ☐ **1 clove garlic, crushed**
- ☐ **1 large orange, segmented**
- ☐ **1 tablespoon chopped fresh parsley**
- ☐ **$^{1}/_{2}$ cup (30 g) soft breadcrumbs**

ORANGE AND TOMATO BUTTER

- ☐ **125 g butter, softened**
- ☐ **3 teaspoons grated orange rind**
- ☐ **1 tablespoon orange juice**
- ☐ **2 teaspoons tomato sauce**

1 Run a knife inside fish across bones, starting from head and working down to the tail to remove bones, taking care not to cut through back. Turn fish and repeat with other side. Cut centre bone at both ends and gently lift out bone.

2 Melt butter in frypan. Cook shallots and garlic for 1-2 minutes. Remove from heat and stir in orange, parsley and breadcrumbs and spread inside fish. Place on a greased sheet of aluminium foil, fold aluminium foil over top and completely seal ends. Barbecue until fish is tender and flesh flakes when tested.

3 To make butter, combine butter, rind, juice and sauce and mix well. Season to taste. Form into a sausage shape on a piece of aluminium foil, wrap and refrigerate until firm. Cut into slices and serve with fish.

Make Orange and Tomato Butter

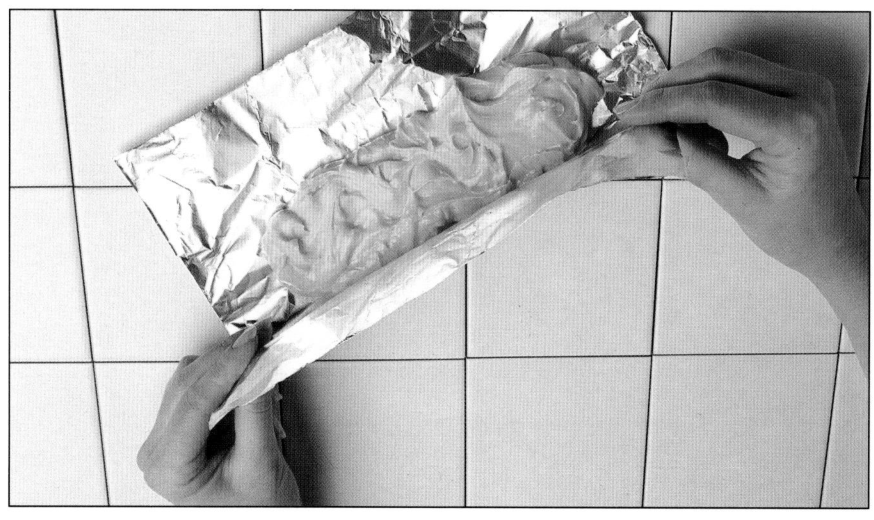

STEAKS WITH BLUE CHEESE AND PORT

If you do not have any port, sweet sherry makes a good substitute.

Serves 6

- ☐ **6 lean fillet steaks**
- ☐ **3 rashers bacon**

FILLING
- ☐ **90 g blue vein cheese**
- ☐ **1 tablespoon cream**
- ☐ **2 teaspoons Dijon-style mustard**
- ☐ **1 clove garlic, crushed**
- ☐ **1 tablespoon port**
- ☐ **1 tablespoon freshly chopped parsley**

1 Trim all visible fat from meat. Cut a pocket in the side of each steak. Combine cheese, cream, mustard, garlic, port and parsley.

2 Push a spoonful of mixture into cut pocket of each steak. Remove rind from bacon, cut each rasher in half and wrap around the side of steaks. Secure with a toothpick. Barbecue or grill on both sides until cooked as desired.

Steaks with Blue Cheese and Port and Pork Fillets with Tangy Apple Sauce

COOK'S TIP

Don't slash steak to see if it is cooked, instead press gently with blunt tongs. Rare steak is springy to the touch, slightly springy when medium and firm when well done.

PORK FILLETS WITH TANGY APPLE SAUCE

Serves 6

- ☐ **6 small pork fillets**
- ☐ **3 tablespoons honey**
- ☐ **2 teaspoons soy sauce**
- ☐ **1 clove garlic, crushed**
- ☐ **2 tablespoons orange juice**
- ☐ **$^1/_4$ teaspoon five spice powder**

TANGY APPLE SAUCE
- ☐ **30 g butter**
- ☐ **1 cooking apple, peeled and finely sliced**
- ☐ **1 tablespoon mango chutney**
- ☐ **3 tablespoons mayonnaise**
- ☐ **1 teaspoon curry powder**
- ☐ **3 tablespoons cream or evaporated skim milk**

1 In a bowl combine fillets with honey, soy sauce, garlic, orange juice and five spice powder and marinate for 15-20 minutes, turning occasionally. Barbecue or grill until tender, brushing with remaining marinade during cooking.

2 To make sauce, melt butter in a frypan. Cook apple for 2-3 minutes or until softened. Place in a food processor bowl with chutney, mayonnaise, curry powder and cream and process until smooth. Spoon over sliced pork fillets.

COOK'S TIP

If using a hotplate to barbecue, heat well before placing the meat on it. When cooking is completed, scrape off any residue so it's clean for the next use. Some barbecue chefs like to clean the hotplate with a glass of wine.

Gingerbread Apricot Upside Down Cake and Fruit Mince Shortcake

Plates, Table and Chairs Mid City Home and Garden

TIME SAVER

Make preheating the oven or griller your first cooking step so that it is ready when you need it.

Tiles Country Floors

GINGERBREAD APRICOT UPSIDE DOWN CAKE

Serves 10

- ☐ 1/2 cup (60 g) dried apricots
- ☐ 60 g butter, softened
- ☐ 1/2 cup (125 g) brown sugar
- ☐ 4 tablespoons chopped pecan nuts

GINGERBREAD

- ☐ 1 cup (125 g) plain flour, sifted
- ☐ 1/2 cup (60 g) self-raising flour, sifted
- ☐ 1/2 teaspoon bicarbonate of soda, sifted
- ☐ 3 teaspoons ground ginger
- ☐ 1/2 teaspoon ground nutmeg
- ☐ 1/2 cup (90 g) brown sugar
- ☐ 1/2 cup (185 g) golden syrup
- ☐ 1/2 cup (125 mL) water
- ☐ 125 g butter

1 Cover apricots with boiling water and soak for 30 minutes. Drain and set aside. Combine butter and sugar in small bowl, mixing until smooth. Spread mixture over a greased and lined 20 cm ring pan. Sprinkle with pecan nuts and top with apricots, cut side up.

2 To make gingerbread, place flours, soda, ginger, nutmeg and sugar in a large bowl. Combine golden syrup, water and butter in saucepan, stirring over low heat until butter is melted. Cool slightly and pour into dry ingredients. Stir until ingredients are well combined. Spoon gingerbread into prepared pan. Bake at 180°C for 35-40 minutes. Stand 15 minutes before turning out ontc a wire rack to cool.

COOK'S TIP

When baking, have eggs at room temperature — this will ensure that baked products gain maximum volume.

FRUIT MINCE SHORTCAKE

Serves 8

- ☐ 2 cups (250 g) self-raising flour
- ☐ 125 g butter
- ☐ 1/2 cup (125 g) caster sugar
- ☐ 1 egg, beaten
- ☐ 1 tablespoon lemon juice
- ☐ 1 cup (200 g) bottled fruit mince
- ☐ 1 egg white, lightly beaten
- ☐ extra caster sugar

1 Sift flour into a large bowl. Rub in butter and stir in sugar, egg and lemon juice, mixing to a firm dough. Cover and refrigerate for 30 minutes.

2 Divide dough in half. Roll out one half large enough to cover base and sides of a greased 20 cm round sandwich pan. Spread fruit mince over base.

3 Roll out remaining dough large enough to cover fruit mince. Press edges together firmly. Brush lightly with egg white and sprinkle with extra caster sugar. Bake at 180°C for 30-35 minutes. Stand 10 minutes before turning out onto a wire rack to cool.

Family FAVOURITES

When you have a yearning for grandma's real home cooking, satisfy your tastebuds with our shortcut classic family favourites.

SWISS VEAL ROAST WITH CREAMY MUSHROOM SAUCE

Serves 4

- ☐ **1 kg boned loin veal**
- ☐ **2 slices wholemeal bread, buttered both sides**
- ☐ **1/2 teaspoon mixed dried herbs**
- ☐ **1/2 cup (60 g) grated Swiss cheese**
- ☐ **2 shallots, finely chopped**
- ☐ **freshly ground black pepper**
- ☐ **30 g butter**
- ☐ **3/4 cup (190 mL) beef stock**
- ☐ **3/4 cup (190 mL) dry white wine**
- ☐ **125 g mushrooms, sliced**
- ☐ **2 teaspoons cornflour blended with 3 tablespoons cream**

1 Trim meat of excess fat and lay out flat on a board. Remove crusts and place bread on the centre of meat. Top with mixed herbs, cheese, shallots and pepper. Roll up and secure with string at 2.5 cm intervals.

2 Melt butter in a baking dish. Add meat and sear well on all sides. Remove from heat. Pour in stock and wine and bake at 180°C for 1 hour or until cooked as desired, basting frequently with pan juices. Remove meat and keep warm.

3 Place baking dish on top of stove, and bring liquid to the boil. Add mushrooms, simmering for 1-2 minutes. Whisk in blended cornflour, stirring until sauce thickens. Slice meat, spoon sauce over and serve.

TIME SAVER

Buying ingredients in the form given in the recipe, such as grated cheese, boned chicken breasts and cubed meat, cuts down on preparation time and makes life easier for you.

CORNED BEEF WITH RASPBERRIES

We have used raspberries in this recipe, however you may use whatever type of berries you like. Why not try blueberries or boysenberries when they are available?

Serves 6

- ☐ **1.5 kg piece corned beef**
- ☐ **2 cups (500 mL) water**
- ☐ **2 cups (500 mL) pineapple juice**
- ☐ **2 tablespoons brown sugar**
- ☐ **1 tablespoon chopped fresh mint**

SAUCE

- ☐ **1 cup (250 mL) beef stock**
- ☐ **3 tablespoons port**
- ☐ **2 teaspoons cornflour blended with a little water**
- ☐ **1 cup (150 g) fresh or frozen raspberries (or any other berries)**
- ☐ **1 teaspoon sugar**

1 Place corned beef in a large saucepan with combined water, pineapple juice, brown sugar and mint. Cover and simmer for 1½ hours. Stand in liquid for 15-20 minutes before serving.

2 To make sauce, combine stock and port in a pan and bring to the boil. Stir in blended cornflour and raspberries. Cook for 2-3 minutes until sauce boils and thickens. Slice meat and serve with sauce.

COOK'S TIP

Corned beef should always be rested in the cooking water for 15-20 minutes before slicing, this makes the meat easier to slice, more tender and juicy.

Oval Platter Made Where *Plates* Mid City Home and Garden

Swiss Veal Roast with Creamy Mushroom Sauce, Corned Beef with Raspberries and Pork Loin with Pineapple Sauce (see page 60)

Cook's Tip

Roast meat should always be rested before carving. Place on a warmed platter, cover with foil and leave to stand for 10-20 minutes. The roast will then be easier to carve, more tender and juicy.

ROAST CHICKEN AND CURRIED RICE STUFFING

Serves 4

- ☐ **1.5 kg chicken**
- ☐ **4 rashers bacon, chopped**
- ☐ **4 shallots, chopped**
- ☐ **2 teaspoons curry powder**
- ☐ **2$^1/_2$ cups (450 g) cooked long-grain rice**
- ☐ **1 cup (60 g) soft breadcrumbs**
- ☐ **1 tablespoon olive oil**

SAUCE

- ☐ **30 g butter**
- ☐ **1 onion, chopped**
- ☐ **1 green capsicum, chopped**
- ☐ **125 g mushrooms, sliced**
- ☐ **440 g canned tomatoes**
- ☐ **2 tablespoons tomato paste**
- ☐ **3 tablespoons red wine**
- ☐ **1 tablespoon sugar**
- ☐ **$^1/_2$ cup (125 mL) water**

1 Wash chicken and pat dry on absorbent paper. Cook bacon, shallots and curry powder in a frypan until bacon is crisp. Remove from heat and stir in rice and breadcrumbs.

2 Fill chicken with rice mixture, securing opening with a skewer. Place in a baking dish, brush with oil and bake at 180°C for 1$^1/_2$ hours, basting frequently with pan juices.

3 To make the sauce, melt butter in a saucepan and cook onion, capsicum and mushrooms for 2-3 minutes. Stir in undrained tomatoes, tomato paste, wine, sugar and water and season to taste.

4 Cook over medium heat for 8-10 minutes until sauce has reduced by a quarter, stirring occasionally. Break chicken into serving portions, spoon sauce over and serve.

TIME SAVER

Precious time can be saved by keeping cooked rice or pasta in the refrigerator or freezer, it is then ready to use in dishes calling for cooked rice or can easily be reheated in the microwave to accompany a meal.

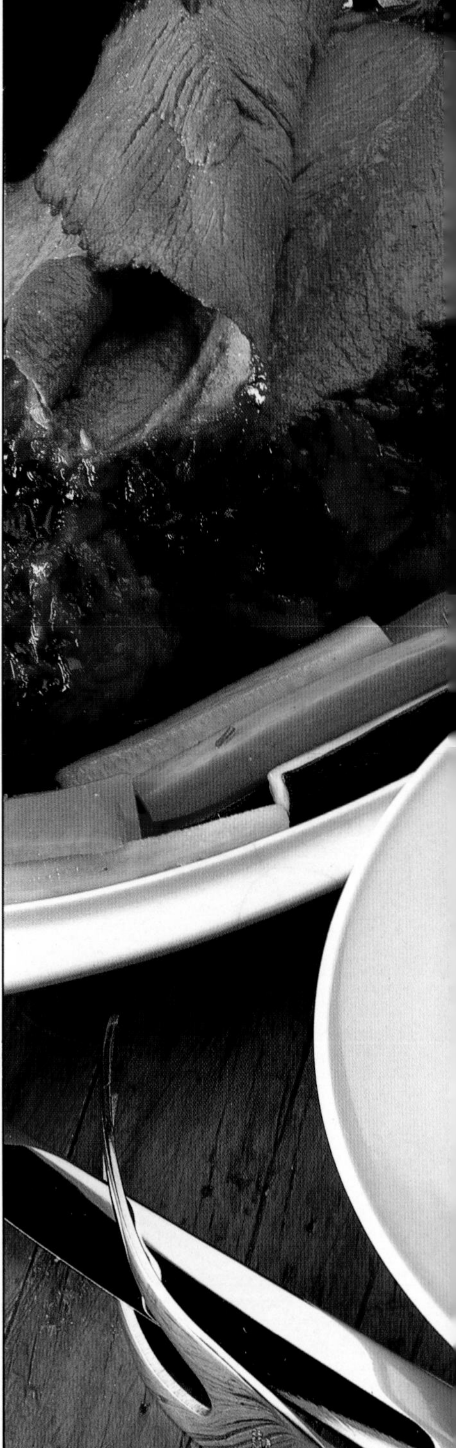

Plates Mid City Home and Garden

Red Currant Lamb Roast and Brandied Beef with Horseradish Sauce

Roast Chicken and Curried Rice Stuffing

Plate Villa Italiana

PORK LOIN WITH PINEAPPLE SAUCE

Serves 6

- ☐ **1.5 kg boned rolled loin pork**
- ☐ **1 teaspoon salt**

PINEAPPLE SAUCE

- ☐ **2$^1/_2$ tablespoons brown sugar**
- ☐ **1$^1/_2$ tablespoons light soy sauce**
- ☐ **225 g canned crushed pineapple**
- ☐ **2 teaspoons grated fresh ginger**
- ☐ **2 teaspoons cornflour blended with 2 tablespoons water**

COOK'S TIP

Simmering beer, wine or spirits, will cause the alcohol content and most of the kilojoules to evaporate, leaving an excellent flavour.

1 Place pork in a lightly oiled baking dish and rub salt well into scored rind. Bake at 250°C for 20 minutes, then reduce heat to 180°C and cook a further 1½ hours until well browned and tender.
2 To make sauce, combine brown sugar, soy sauce, pineapple and ginger and pour over pork during the last 20 minutes of cooking, basting with sauce occasionally.
3 Remove pork from dish and keep warm in a low oven. Skim excess fat from pan juices. Whisk in blended cornflour and water, stir over heat until sauce boils and thickens. Slice pork and serve with sauce.

RED CURRANT LAMB ROAST

Serves 6

- ☐ **1.5 kg lean leg lamb**

BASTE
- ☐ **30 g butter**
- ☐ **1 teaspoon grated fresh ginger**
- ☐ **1 clove garlic, crushed**
- ☐ **1 teaspoon soy sauce**
- ☐ **1 tablespoon red currant jelly**

SAUCE
- ☐ **2 tablespoons red currant jelly**
- ☐ **1 cup (250 mL) chicken stock**
- ☐ **2 tablespoons chopped fresh mint**
- ☐ **1 tablespoon cornflour blended with 3 tablespoons port**

1 Trim meat of excess fat and place in a baking dish. To make baste, combine butter, ginger, garlic, soy sauce and 1 tablespoon redcurrant jelly in a saucepan. Stir over medium heat until butter melts.
2 Pour over lamb and bake at 180°C for 1¼-1½ hours until cooked as desired, basting frequently with pan liquid. Remove meat and keep warm.
3 To make sauce, place baking dish on top of stove. Combine redcurrant jelly, stock and mint. Bring to the boil, whisk in blended cornflour, stirring until sauce thickens. Slice meat and serve with sauce.

BRANDIED BEEF WITH HORSERADISH SAUCE

Serves 6

- ☐ **1.5 kg beef fillet**
- ☐ **freshly ground black pepper**
- ☐ **30 g butter**
- ☐ **3 tablespoons brandy**

HORSERADISH SAUCE
- ☐ **½ cup (125 mL) mayonnaise**
- ☐ **½ cup (125 mL) unflavoured yoghurt**
- ☐ **1 teaspoon lemon juice**
- ☐ **1 teaspoon horseradish relish**
- ☐ **1 avocado, peeled, stoned and chopped**

1 Trim all visible fat from meat and sprinkle with pepper. Tie with string at even intervals so it will keep its shape during cooking. Heat butter over high heat in a baking dish and sear meat on all sides until golden brown. Spoon brandy over meat and bake at 180°C for 25-35 minutes until cooked as desired, basting frequently with pan juices.
2 To make sauce combine mayonnaise, yoghurt, lemon juice, horseradish and avocado in the bowl of a food processor or blender. Process until thoroughly combined. Slice beef and serve with sauce.

COOK'S TIP

To sear a rolled roast, heat butter or oil in pan, add meat and roll back and forth to brown on all sides.

Veal and Scalloped Potato Casserole and Tomato and Beef Casserole with Sesame Seed Topping

VEAL AND SCALLOPED POTATO CASSEROLE

For a change, use chicken fillets in place of the veal in this recipe.

Serves 4

- ☐ **4 medium veal steaks**
- ☐ **2 tablespoons olive oil**

SAUCE
- ☐ **125 g mushrooms, sliced**
- ☐ **1 clove garlic, crushed**
- ☐ **3 shallots, chopped**
- ☐ **1 teaspoon French mustard**
- ☐ **$^3/_4$ cup (190 mL) chicken stock**
- ☐ **2 teaspoons cornflour blended with $^1/_2$ cup (125 mL) cream or evaporated skim milk**
- ☐ **4 large potatoes, thinly sliced**
- ☐ **3 tablespoons cream**
- ☐ **$^3/_4$ cup (90 g) grated tasty cheese**

1 Trim meat of all visible fat. Heat oil in a frypan, cook meat until brown on both sides. Transfer to an ovenproof casserole dish.

2 To make sauce, add mushrooms, garlic and shallots to the pan. Cook until mushrooms are soft and place on top of meat. Combine mustard and stock, pour into the pan and bring to the boil, season to taste. Whisk in blended cornflour and stir over heat until sauce thickens. Spoon over meat and vegetable layer.

3 Top with potato slices pour over cream, cover and bake at 180°C for 30 minutes. Uncover and sprinkle cheese over potato, cook a further 30 minutes until cheese is golden and meat tender.

TOMATO AND BEEF CASSEROLE WITH SESAME SEED TOPPING

Serves 4

BURGERS
- ☐ **500 g minced topside steak**
- ☐ **1 clove garlic, crushed**
- ☐ **1 onion, chopped**
- ☐ **1 egg, beaten**
- ☐ **4 tablespoons instant oats**
- ☐ **1 tablespoon oyster sauce**
- ☐ **1 tablespoon tomato sauce**
- ☐ **2 tablespoons olive oil**

SAUCE
- ☐ **1 onion, chopped**
- ☐ **440 g canned tomatoes**
- ☐ **2 tablespoons tomato paste**
- ☐ **$^1/_2$ teaspoon sugar**
- ☐ **2 teaspoons cornflour blended with water**

TOPPING
- ☐ **5 slices bread, buttered, crusts removed**
- ☐ **2 tablespoons sesame seeds**

1 To make burgers, combine mince, garlic, onion, egg, oats and sauces and shape into eight hamburgers. Heat oil in a frypan and cook hamburgers until well browned on both sides. Transfer to an ovenproof casserole dish. Drain pan.

2 To make sauce, add onion to pan and cook for 2-3 minutes until soft. Mash undrained tomatoes and combine with tomato paste and sugar. Pour into the pan, stir over heat until boiling. Whisk in blended cornflour and cook until mixture thickens. Pour over meat in casserole.

3 To make topping, cut buttered bread into cubes and arrange over sauce. Sprinkle with sesame seeds and bake at 180°C for 35-40 minutes or until topping is golden.

BLUE VEIN BEEF CASSEROLE

Serves 4

- ☐ **750 g boneless blade steak**
- ☐ **2 tablespoons olive oil**
- ☐ **1 cup (250 mL) beef stock**
- ☐ **1/2 cup (125 mL) tomato puree**
- ☐ **2 tablespoons port**
- ☐ **1/4 teaspoon ground cumin**
- ☐ **1 cinnamon stick**
- ☐ **12 small white onions**
- ☐ **90 g blue vein cheese, cut into 1 cm cubes**

1 Trim meat of all visible fat and cut into 5 cm cubes. Heat oil in a frypan and cook meat until brown. Transfer to an ovenproof casserole dish.

2 Add stock, tomato puree, port, cumin and cinnamon stick to the pan, season to taste. Bring to the boil and pour over meat, cover and bake at 180°C for 1 hour.

3 Place onions in a saucepan of water, bring to the boil. Boil for 2-3 minutes, drain, add to meat and cook a further 30 minutes. Top casserole with blue vein cheese. Stand 10 minutes before serving.

COOK'S TIP

When cutting meat or poultry into cubes for casseroles etc, cut across the grain in approximately 2.5 cm pieces. This will ensure that the meat is tender when cooked.

COTTAGE PIE

It's always a problem knowing what to do with leftover roast meat. This version of the traditional cottage pie solves all those worries in next to no time.

Serves 4

- ☐ **400 g cold cooked meat (lamb or beef etc), finely chopped**
- ☐ **1 onion, grated**
- ☐ **1 tablespoon tomato sauce**
- ☐ **1 tablespoon chopped fresh parsley**
- ☐ **1 teaspoon dried thyme**
- ☐ **1/2 teaspoon dried sage**
- ☐ **1/2 teaspoon dried oregano**
- ☐ **1 tomato, sliced**
- ☐ **125 g instant dried potato flakes**
- ☐ **1 cup (250 mL) boiling water**
- ☐ **1/2 cup (125 mL) milk**
- ☐ **30 g melted butter**
- ☐ **1/2 cup (30 g) crushed potato crisps**

1 Combine meat, onion, sauce, parsley and herbs, season to taste. Spoon into a 20 cm ovenproof dish and top with tomato slices.

2 Combine instant potato, water, milk and butter; spread on top of meat. Sprinkle with crushed crisps and cook at 200°C for 20-25 minutes. Allow to stand for 5 minutes before serving.

MICROWAVE IT

For an even faster meal you can easily make the Cottage Pie in the microwave. Use a 20 cm microwave-safe dish and cook on HIGH (100%) for 4-5 minutes, stand 5 minutes before serving.

Blue Vein Beef Casserole and Cottage Pie

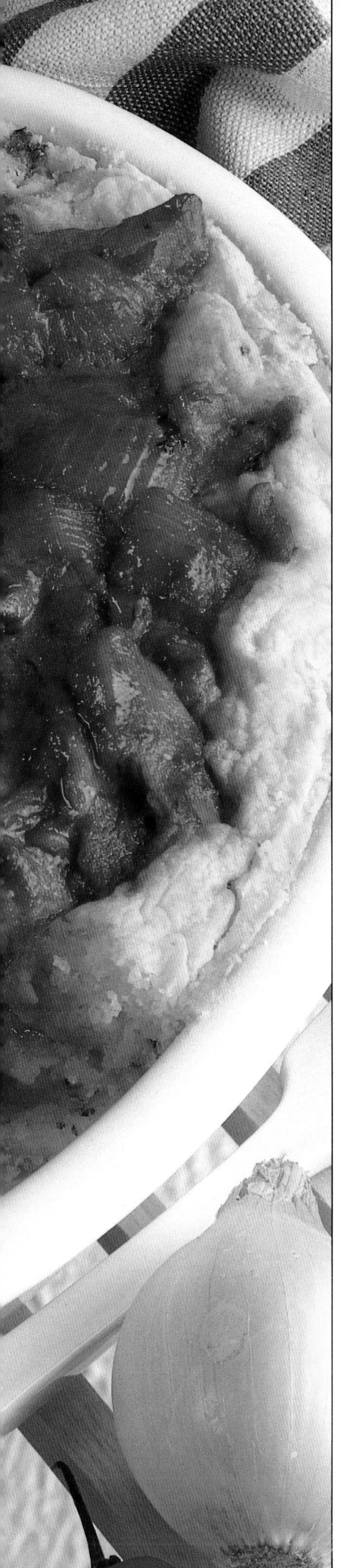

STEP-BY-STEP

CRUSTY CHICKEN GOULASH

Serves 4

FILLING
- ☐ **2 tablespoons polyunsaturated oil**
- ☐ **2 large onions, chopped**
- ☐ **500 g chicken fillets, cut into thin strips**
- ☐ **1 1/2 tablespoons paprika**
- ☐ **2 tablespoons seasoned plain flour**
- ☐ **1 tablespoon tomato paste**
- ☐ **1/2 cup (125 mL) red wine**
- ☐ **1/2 cup (125 mL) chicken stock**
- ☐ **3 tablespoons unflavoured yoghurt**

CRUST
- ☐ **125 g butter, softened**
- ☐ **300 g sour cream**
- ☐ **1 egg**
- ☐ **1 cup (125 g) self-raising flour**
- ☐ **1 tablespoon chopped fresh parsley**

1 To make filling, heat half the oil in a frypan. Cook onions for 2-3 minutes until golden, remove from pan and set aside. Coat chicken in combined paprika and seasoned flour.

2 Heat remaining oil in pan. Cook chicken for 2-3 minutes. Return onions to pan, stir in combined tomato paste, wine and stock. Bring to the boil, stirring constantly, reduce heat and simmer covered for 6-7 minutes. Remove from heat and stir in yoghurt.

3 To make crust, combine butter, sour cream and egg in a bowl. Stir in sifted flour and parsley, mixing until well combined. To assemble, place mixture in a 2 litre greased casserole, working mixture up to cover sides and base of dish. Spoon in filling, cover and bake at 180°C for 35 minutes. Uncover and bake a further 10 minutes.

Make crust

Press into a 2 litre greased casserole

Spoon filling into crust

Crusty Chicken Goulash

Tiles Pazotti Tiles

Salmon Rice and Spinach Loaf

SALMON RICE AND SPINACH LOAF

Serves 4

- ☐ **9 spinach leaves, stalks removed**
- ☐ **440 g canned salmon, drained**
- ☐ **3 eggs**
- ☐ **3 tablespoons sour cream or unflavoured yoghurt**
- ☐ **2 tablespoons mayonnaise**
- ☐ **1 tablespoon lemon juice**
- ☐ **$^{1}/_{2}$ cup (90 g) cooked rice**
- ☐ **2 tablespoons grated Parmesan cheese**

1 Wet spinach leaves and boil or steam until soft.

2 Line the base and sides of a greased ovenproof 9 cm x 22 cm loaf pan with half of the spinach leaves, allow some of the leaves to hang over the sides of the pan.

3 Squeeze excess moisture from remaining leaves. Chop and combine with all the remaining ingredients, season to taste. Spoon salmon mixture into spinach lined dish. Enclose with the overhanging spinach leaves, cover and cook at 200°C for 45 minutes or until firm. Stand for 10 minutes before serving.

MICROWAVE IT

This loaf cooks quickly in the microwave. Remember to use a microwave-safe loaf dish. Preparation of the loaf is the same. Cover, then cook on HIGH (100%) for 13 minutes, stand 5 minutes before serving.

CURRIED TUNA LASAGNE

This recipe freezes well. Thaw overnight in the refrigerator before cooking.

Serves 6

- ☐ **9 sheets instant lasagne noodles**
- ☐ **425 g canned tuna, drained and flaked**
- ☐ **15 g butter**
- ☐ **2 stalks celery, finely chopped**
- ☐ **1 onion, chopped**

SAUCE

- ☐ **30 g butter**
- ☐ **4 tablespoons plain flour**
- ☐ **2 teaspoons curry powder**
- ☐ **$2^{1}/_{4}$ cups (560 mL) milk**
- ☐ **$^{3}/_{4}$ cup (190 mL) water**
- ☐ **2 eggs, beaten**
- ☐ **2 tablespoons grated tasty cheese**

Plates Villeroy & Boch

TOPPING

- 2 tablespoons grated tasty cheese
- 1 teaspoon curry powder
- 1/2 teaspoon paprika

1 To make sauce, melt butter in a saucepan. Stir in flour and curry powder and cook for 2-3 minutes. Remove from heat, whisk in combined milk and water. Stir over heat until sauce boils and thickens. Blend in egg mixture and cheese.

2 Spoon a little sauce over the base of a shallow ovenproof dish. Top with three lasagne sheets and spread over half the tuna.

3 Melt butter in a frypan and cook celery and onion until onion is soft. Spread half over tuna, top with a layer of sauce. Repeat layers finishing with noodles then sauce.

4 To make topping, combine cheese, curry powder and paprika. Sprinkle over top and bake at 190°C for 30-35 minutes or until tender.

TIME SAVER

Make preheating the oven or griller your first cooking step so that it is ready when you need it.

WHOLEMEAL SPAGHETTI WITH TOMATOES AND ASPARAGUS

Serves 4

- **500 g wholemeal spaghetti**

SAUCE

- **1 tablespoon olive oil**
- **1 clove garlic, crushed**
- **425 g canned tomatoes, drained and chopped**
- **300 g canned asparagus cuts, drained**
- **1 tablespoon chopped fresh parsley**
- **1 tablespoon brown sugar**
- **2 tablespoons red wine**

1 Cook spaghetti in boiling water following the packet instructions. Drain and keep warm.

2 To make sauce, melt oil in a frypan, cook garlic for 1 minute. Stir in tomatoes, asparagus, parsley, sugar and wine and season to taste. Cover and simmer for 15-20 minutes. Spoon sauce over hot spaghetti and serve with Parmesan cheese if desired.

COOK'S TIP

Parsley will keep fresh for several weeks by washing and storing in a sealed container in the refrigerator.

Curried Tuna Lasagne and Wholemeal Spaghetti with Tomatoes and Asparagus

Cook's Tip

If the mixture is too sticky to handle, add $1\frac{1}{2}$ tablespoons self raising flour to salmon mixture.

Salmon Croquettes

SALMON CROQUETTES

Plate Villeroy & Boch

Serves 4

- ☐ **3 large potatoes, cooked and mashed**
- ☐ **1 onion, grated**
- ☐ **440 g canned pink salmon, drained and flaked**
- ☐ **1 teaspoon Dijon-style mustard**
- ☐ **2 tablespoons mayonnaise**
- ☐ **1 egg, beaten**
- ☐ **200 g cheese flavoured biscuits, crushed**
- ☐ **polyunsaturated oil for cooking**

1 Combine potato, onion, salmon, mustard, mayonnaise and egg, season to taste. Shape mixture into croquettes and roll in biscuit crumbs to coat.

2 Heat oil in a frypan. Cook croquettes over medium heat until golden brown. Drain on absorbent paper.

HERB SCHNITZELS WITH VERMOUTH SAUCE

Plate Villa Italiana Statue Mid City Home and Garden

Serves 4

- ☐ **4 lean medium veal schnitzels**
- ☐ **3 tablespoons lemon juice**
- ☐ **3 tablespoons dry vermouth**
- ☐ **3 tablespoons polyunsaturated oil**
- ☐ **plain flour**
- ☐ **1 egg, beaten**
- ☐ **$\frac{3}{4}$ cup (90 g) dry breadcrumbs**
- ☐ **1 tablespoon chopped fresh rosemary**
- ☐ **1 tablespoon chopped fresh parsley**
- ☐ **30 g butter**
- ☐ **2 teaspoons cornflour blended with $\frac{1}{2}$ cup (125 mL) cream or evaporated skim milk**

1 Trim meat of all visible fat and place in a shallow dish. Combine lemon juice, vermouth and 2 tablespoons oil. Pour over meat and marinate for 10-15 minutes.

2 Drain meat and reserve marinade. Coat schnitzels in flour, dip in beaten egg, then coat in combined breadcrumbs, rosemary and parsley.

3 Heat butter and 1 tablespoon oil in a frypan. Cook schnitzels on both sides until golden brown. Remove from pan and keep warm.

4 Drain pan. Pour in reserved marinade and bring to the boil. Boil until liquid has reduced by half, whisk in blended cornflour and cream stirring over heat until sauce thickens. Spoon sauce over schnitzels and serve.

Herb Schnitzels with Vermouth Sauce

Microwave It

Combine chicken, onion and garlic in a microwave-safe bowl. Cook on HIGH (100%) for 8 minutes, stir twice during cooking. Add seasoning mix, water and taco sauce, cook on HIGH (100%) for a further 8 minutes.

Plates Pillivuyt, Hale Imports

Macaroni Cheese and Cabanossi and Chicken Tacos

MACARONI CHEESE AND CABANOSSI

Cabanossi, a delicious Italian sausage, is available from supermarkets and delicatessens. If you prefer, it can be replaced by any spicy sausage.

Serves 4

- ☐ **30 g butter**
- ☐ **4 shallots, chopped**
- ☐ **$^1/_2$ red capsicum, finely chopped**
- ☐ **125 g mushrooms, sliced**
- ☐ **3 sticks cabanossi sausage, sliced**
- ☐ **4 cups (500 g) cooked macaroni pasta**

SAUCE

- ☐ **60 g butter**
- ☐ **3 tablespoons plain flour**
- ☐ **$1^1/_3$ cups (330 mL) milk**
- ☐ **1 teaspoon French mustard**
- ☐ **3 tablespoons cream or evaporated skim milk**
- ☐ **3 tablespoons grated Parmesan cheese**
- ☐ **1 cup (125 g) grated tasty cheese**
- ☐ **paprika**

1 Place butter, shallots, capsicum, mushrooms and cabanossi in a saucepan. Cook for 2-3 minutes, remove and set aside.

2 To make sauce, melt butter in pan, add flour and cook for 1 minute. Pour in combined milk, mustard and cream. Cook, for 3-4 minutes, stirring all the time, until sauce boils and thickens. Mix in Parmesan cheese.

3 Combine macaroni, mushroom mixture and sauce. Spoon into a lightly greased shallow ovenproof dish, top with tasty cheese and dust lightly with paprika. Bake at 200°C for 10 minutes until cheese melts.

Cook's Tip

$1^1/_2$ cups (180 g) uncooked dried pasta will give you 4 cups (500 g) cooked pasta.

CHICKEN TACOS

Serves 4

- ☐ **1 tablespoon polyunsaturated oil**
- ☐ **500 g chicken, minced**
- ☐ **1 large onion, finely chopped**
- ☐ **2 cloves garlic, crushed**
- ☐ **2 tablespoons (or 35 g packet) taco seasoning mix**
- ☐ **$^1/_2$ cup (125 mL) water**
- ☐ **3 tablespoons taco sauce**
- ☐ **8 taco shells**
- ☐ **grated tasty cheese**

1 Heat oil in a frypan. Add chicken, onion and garlic and cook over medium heat for 5-6 minutes. Stir in seasoning mix, water and taco sauce, cook a further 4-5 minutes.

2 Place taco shells on an oven tray and warm through in a moderate oven. Fill shells with taco filling, top with cheese and serve with extra taco sauce and salad if desired.

DINNER AND DASH

Combine these tasty light meals with your hectic timetable when you have to eat and run.

ZUCCHINI AND SALMON SOUFFLES

Serves 4

- ☐ **2 large zucchini, grated**
- ☐ **$^{1}/_{2}$ cup (125 g) sour cream or unflavoured yoghurt**
- ☐ **1 teaspoon chilli sauce**
- ☐ **220 g canned salmon, drained**
- ☐ **2 egg yolks**
- ☐ **2 egg whites**

1 Blend sour cream, chilli sauce, salmon and egg yolks in a food processor, season to taste and stir into zucchini.

2 Beat egg whites until stiff peaks form, fold through zucchini mixture. Spoon into four individual souffle dishes about $1^{1}/_{2}$ cup capacity and cook at 200°C for 25 minutes or until puffed and golden.

MICROWAVE IT

Spoon mixture into four individual microwave-safe dishes. Cook on MEDIUM/HIGH (70%) for 7 minutes or until just set in the centre. Stand 5 minutes before serving.

SKEWERED SEAFOOD WITH BASIL AND CHIVE BUTTER

Serves 4

- ☐ **150 g scallops, halved**
- ☐ **2 fish fillets, skin and bones removed, cut into cubes**
- ☐ **250 g cooked prawns, shelled and deveined**

BASIL AND CHIVE BUTTER

- ☐ **125 g butter, softened**
- ☐ **2 tablespoons chopped fresh basil**
- ☐ **2 tablespoons chopped chives**
- ☐ **1 tablespoon lemon juice**

1 Thread seafood onto eight oiled bamboo skewers alternating scallops, fish and prawns.

2 To make butter, combine butter, basil, chives and lemon juice, season to taste. Brush seafood with butter and grill for 3-4 minutes each side, basting frequently.

SALMON SALAD ROLLUP

Serves 4

- ☐ **250 g cream cheese**
- ☐ **$^{1}/_{2}$ bunch chives, chopped**
- ☐ **2 tablespoons lemon juice**
- ☐ **4 rounds pita bread**
- ☐ **shredded lettuce**
- ☐ **sliced red and green capsicums**
- ☐ **1 onion, chopped**
- ☐ **440 g canned salmon, drained**

1 Beat cream cheese until soft, mix in chives and lemon juice. Season to taste and spread cream cheese mixture over bread rounds.

2 Arrange shredded lettuce, sliced capsicums and onion over cheese mixture. Top with flaked salmon, roll up and serve.

COOK'S TIP

Remember to use leftovers in soups, casseroles, sandwiches or salads.

Zucchini and Salmon Souffles, Skewered Seafood with Basil and Chive Butter and Salmon Salad Rollup

Cook's Tip

If using bamboo skewers, soak in cold water for an hour or so before threading with food. This prevents them from splintering and burning and stops food from sticking to the skewers. Oil after soaking.

FLORENTINE BURGERS

Plates Pillivuyt, Hale Imports *Tiles* Pazotti Tiles

You will find packaged pita bread is available in most supermarkets. It is a smaller version of the Lebanese flat bread.

Serves 4

- ☐ **500 g lean minced topside steak**
- ☐ **1 egg, beaten**
- ☐ **1 teaspoon mixed herbs**
- ☐ **1 cup (100 g) instant oats**
- ☐ **1 onion, grated**
- ☐ **2 tablespoons olive oil**
- ☐ **4 spinach leaves, stalks removed and shredded**
- ☐ **30 g butter**
- ☐ **4 eggs**
- ☐ **4 pita pocket bread rounds, buttered**

1 Combine mince, egg, herbs, oats and onion, season to taste. Shape into four large patties. Heat oil in a frypan and cook patties for 6-8 minutes or until golden brown on both sides, remove from pan and keep warm.

2 Add spinach to pan, stir over heat for 2-3 minutes. Remove and keep warm.

Florentine Burgers, Ham and Asparagus Rolls with Lemon Mustard and Chicken and Melon Kebabs

Melt butter in pan and fry eggs to desired preference.

3 Serve a spoonful of spinach on each bread round, top with a meat patty and egg.

HAM AND ASPARAGUS ROLLS WITH LEMON MUSTARD

Serves 4

- ☐ **340 g canned asparagus spears**
- ☐ **8 slices sandwich ham**

LEMON MUSTARD SAUCE

- ☐ **30 g melted butter**
- ☐ **2 tablespoons plain flour**
- ☐ **1 cup (250 mL) chicken stock**
- ☐ **1 tablespoon lemon juice**
- ☐ **1 teaspoon mustard seed**
- ☐ **1 teaspoon French mustard**
- ☐ **3 tablespoons cream or evaporated skim milk**

1 Drain asparagus and place 2-3 spears on each slice of ham. Roll up and arrange seam side down in a shallow ovenproof dish.

2 To make sauce, melt butter in a saucepan, add flour and cook, stirring for 1 minute. Stir in combined stock, lemon juice, mustard seed and mustard. Cook for 3-4 minutes or until sauce boils and thickens. Remove from heat. Whisk in cream and pour over ham rolls in dish, bake at 200°C for 10-15 minutes or until heated through.

MICROWAVE IT

These rolls are easy to cook in the microwave. Prepare ham rolls as for conventional recipe then arrange in a shallow microwave-safe dish. To make sauce, combine butter and flour in a microwave-safe bowl, cook on HIGH (100%) for 1 minute. Stir in stock, lemon juice, mustard seed and mustard, cook on HIGH (100%) for 4 minutes, stirring twice during cooking. Pour sauce over ham rolls then cook on HIGH (100%) for 2-3 minutes.

Mixed Vegetable Omelette

CHICKEN AND MELON KEBABS

We have used fruit salad yoghurt in this recipe, however you may use any low-fat fruit flavoured yoghurt in its place.

Serves 4

- ☐ **6 chicken fillets, cut into 2.5 cm cubes**
- ☐ **1/2 rockmelon, cubed**

BASTE

- ☐ **200 g low-fat fruit salad yoghurt**
- ☐ **1/2 teaspoon cinnamon**
- ☐ **1 clove garlic, crushed**
- ☐ **2 tablespoons orange juice**

1 Alternate chicken and melon cubes onto eight oiled bamboo skewers.

2 To make baste, combine yoghurt, cinnamon, garlic and juice and brush over kebabs. Stand for 5 minutes. Grill kebabs for 4-5 minutes each side, basting frequently.

MIXED VEGETABLE OMELETTE

Serves 2

- ☐ **90 g butter**
- ☐ **1 leek, washed and sliced**
- ☐ **1 1/2 cups (375 g) finely chopped mixed vegetables of your choice**
- ☐ **1 clove garlic, crushed**
- ☐ **1 teaspoon mustard seed**
- ☐ **6 eggs**
- ☐ **3 tablespoons water**

1 Melt 60 g butter in a frypan, add leek, vegetables, garlic and mustard seed. Stir over medium heat for 5 minutes or until vegetables are just tender, remove from pan and keep warm.

2 Beat eggs and water together until fluffy, season to taste. Melt remaining butter in pan. Pour in half the egg mixture and cook until set. Spoon half the vegetable mixture onto omelette and fold over. Repeat with remaining egg mixture and vegetables.

TIME SAVER

Using some of the frozen mixed vegetable varieties for this recipe cuts down on preparation time as the chopping of the vegetables is eliminated. The cooking times will remain the same.

ORIENTAL PRAWN CREPES

Serves 4

- ☐ **1 tablespoon polyunsaturated oil**
- ☐ **250 g tofu, cubed**
- ☐ **4 shallots, chopped**
- ☐ **4 tablespoons chopped red capsicum**
- ☐ **1 clove garlic, crushed**
- ☐ **1 cup (50 g) bean sprouts**
- ☐ **1 tablespoon soy sauce**
- ☐ **1 tablespoon plum sauce**
- ☐ **200 g cooked prawns, shelled and deveined**
- ☐ **8 prepared crepes (page 43)**

1 Heat oil in a frypan and cook tofu until lightly browned. Toss in shallots, capsicum, garlic and bean sprouts, cook for 1 minute.

2 Stir in soy sauce, plum sauce and prawns, cook until just heated through. Spoon filling into centre of warmed crepes. Roll up and serve with extra plum sauce if desired.

FISH FILLETS TROPICANA

Serves 4

- ☐ **425 g canned mango slices, drained**
- ☐ **4 fish fillets**
- ☐ **2 tablespoons cornflour**
- ☐ **$^{1}/_{2}$ cup (30 g) fresh breadcrumbs**
- ☐ **3 tablespoons coconut**
- ☐ **2 tablespoons chopped macadamia nuts**
- ☐ **2 tablespoons polyunsaturated oil**

1 Puree mango slices in a blender or processor. Coat fillets with cornflour, dip into mango puree and coat with combined breadcrumbs, coconut and nuts.

2 Heat oil in a frypan, cook fish for 3-4 minutes each side or until fish flakes when tested. Remove from pan. Drain on absorbent kitchen paper and serve.

MICROWAVE IT

Cook these delicious fish fillets in the microwave. While you are making the coating and preparing the fish, heat the browning dish for 7 minutes on HIGH (100%). Then add the oil and fish fillets. Cook on HIGH (100%) for 3 minutes, turning once halfway through cooking.

Oriental Prawn Crepes and Fish Fillets Tropicana

Plates Mid City Home and Garden

Quick and Easy Lamb Parcels and Spicy Sausage and Vegetable Stir-fry

QUICK AND EASY LAMB PARCELS

Serves 4

- ☐ **4 large lean lamb leg steaks**
- ☐ **1 onion, sliced**
- ☐ **2 tablespoons chopped parsley**

MARINADE

- ☐ **3 tablespoons tomato sauce**
- ☐ **2 teaspoons soy sauce**
- ☐ **1 tablespoon brown sugar**
- ☐ **1 teaspoon cider vinegar**

1 Trim all visible fat from meat. To make marinade, combine sauces, sugar and vinegar, marinate meat for 15-20 minutes.

2 Place each steak and a little sauce on a sheet of aluminium foil large enough to enclose it completely. Sprinkle 2 teaspoons parsley and a few onion rings over each steak. Wrap steaks tightly in foil. Barbecue or grill until cooked as desired.

COOK'S TIP

When barbecueing, do not turn meat with a fork as it pierces the sealed surfaces, releasing the juices and drying out the meat. Use tongs for turning instead.

SPICY SAUSAGE AND VEGETABLE STIR-FRY

Serves 4

- ☐ **1 tablespoon oil**
- ☐ **500 g Polish sausages, cut into 1 cm thick diagonal slices**
- ☐ **1 clove garlic, crushed**
- ☐ **1 teaspoon grated fresh ginger**
- ☐ **150 g snow peas**
- ☐ **2 carrots, cut into thin strips**
- ☐ **1 red capsicum, cut into thin strips**
- ☐ **4 shallots, cut into 5 cm lengths**
- ☐ **$^{1}/_{2}$ cup (30 g) bean sprouts**
- ☐ **3 tablespoons chicken stock**
- ☐ **2 tablespoons oyster sauce**
- ☐ **$^{1}/_{4}$ teaspoon cumin powder**

1 Heat oil in a frypan or wok. Stir-fry sausage slices for 1-2 minutes and remove from pan. Add garlic and ginger to pan, stir-fry for 1 minute.

2 Stir in snow peas, carrots, capsicum, shallots and sprouts, cook for 2-3 minutes. Pour in combined stock, oyster sauce and cumin powder and cook for 3-4 minutes, or until vegetables are just tender.

3 Return sausages to pan, toss for 1 minute to heat through. Serve accompanied with noodles.

COOK'S TIP

Polish sausage has a spicy flavour and is available at most supermarkets and delicatessens.

The No Time To Shop PANTRY CHECK LIST

Set aside some time each week to plan your family's meals for the week ahead. If you draw up a master grocery list as you go, you will always have all the ingredients you need to create delicious meals for family and friends.

We have included the following pantry check list as a handy reminder to make your shopping easier and quicker.

STAPLE ITEMS
- ☐ baking powder
- ☐ bicarbonate of soda
- ☐ bran
- ☐ breadcrumbs, dried
- ☐ brown sugar
- ☐ caster sugar
- ☐ cocoa
- ☐ coconut
- ☐ coffee
- ☐ cream of tartar
- ☐ dried fruits
- ☐ flour
- ☐ gelatine
- ☐ granulated sugar
- ☐ icing sugar
- ☐ nuts
- ☐ rolled oats
- ☐ stock cubes
- ☐ tea

BISCUITS
- ☐ un-iced plain
- ☐ water crackers

BREADS
- ☐ pita bread
- ☐ sliced white or brown

CANNED FOODS
- ☐ asparagus spears
- ☐ baked beans
- ☐ corn kernels
- ☐ evaporated milk
- ☐ fruit such as pineapple, peaches, apricots
- ☐ salmon
- ☐ spaghetti
- ☐ tomatoes, whole peeled or pureed
- ☐ tomato paste
- ☐ tuna

DAIRY PRODUCTS
- ☐ butter
- ☐ cheese
- ☐ cream
- ☐ eggs
- ☐ milk
- ☐ yoghurt

FROZEN FOODS
- ☐ filo pastry
- ☐ ice cream
- ☐ puff pastry
- ☐ vegetables such as corn, peas, beans

HERBS AND SPICES
- ☐ basil leaves
- ☐ black pepper, ground
- ☐ cayenne pepper
- ☐ chilli powder
- ☐ cinnamon, ground
- ☐ coriander, ground
- ☐ curry powder
- ☐ dill leaves
- ☐ ginger, ground
- ☐ mixed dried herbs
- ☐ mixed spice, ground
- ☐ nutmeg, ground
- ☐ oregano, leaves
- ☐ paprika
- ☐ rosemary leaves
- ☐ sage, ground
- ☐ tarragon leaves
- ☐ thyme, dried

PASTA AND RICE
- ☐ lasagne noodles
- ☐ macaroni
- ☐ rice, white and brown
- ☐ spaghetti, wholemeal or plain

RELISHES, JAMS AND SPREADS
- ☐ chutney
- ☐ golden syrup
- ☐ honey
- ☐ jams such as apricot, plum, strawberry
- ☐ lemon butter
- ☐ peanut butter
- ☐ pickles

SAUCES AND MUSTARDS
- ☐ chilli sauce
- ☐ cranberry sauce
- ☐ plum sauce
- ☐ soy sauce
- ☐ Tabasco sauce
- ☐ tomato sauce
- ☐ Worcestershire sauce
- ☐ Dijon style mustard
- ☐ French mustard
- ☐ wholegrain mustard

SMALLGOODS
- ☐ bacon rashers
- ☐ gherkins, pickled onions
- ☐ ham
- ☐ olives
- ☐ salami

VINEGARS AND OILS
- ☐ olive oil
- ☐ salad dressings
- ☐ sesame oil
- ☐ vinegar, white, brown, cider

FRUIT AND VEGETABLES
- ☐ apples
- ☐ apricots
- ☐ avocado
- ☐ bananas
- ☐ beans
- ☐ broccoli
- ☐ brussels sprouts
- ☐ cabbage
- ☐ capsicum
- ☐ carrots
- ☐ celery
- ☐ cucumber
- ☐ egg plant (aubergine)
- ☐ grapes
- ☐ grapefruit
- ☐ kiwifruit
- ☐ leeks
- ☐ lemons
- ☐ lettuce
- ☐ limes
- ☐ mandarins
- ☐ melons, such as watermelon, cantaloupe, rockmelon
- ☐ mushrooms
- ☐ nectarines
- ☐ onions
- ☐ oranges
- ☐ parsnips
- ☐ peaches
- ☐ pears
- ☐ peas
- ☐ plums
- ☐ potatoes
- ☐ pumpkin
- ☐ shallots (spring onions)
- ☐ spinach
- ☐ strawberries
- ☐ tomatoes
- ☐ turnips
- ☐ zucchini (courgette)

TEN NO NONSENSE NUTRITION TIPS

Nutrition is vitally important for good health, not simply for prevention of illnesses such as heart disease or cancer, but as an energy-boosting tool in your life. You and your family cannot live in top gear on poor foods, just as a car won't perform well on the wrong fuel.

While no diet can guarantee "super health", there is no doubt that good nutrition will help you feel more vital, control your weight, avoid fatigue and improve your immune system.

Unlike fitness or relaxation techniques, eating well requires only minor changes to become part of a daily schedule. Start today to incorporate the following nutrition guidelines into your life.

1 Balance is one of the keys to healthy eating. Every day, you need at least four serves of bread and cereals; four serves of vegetables and fruit; one serve of lean meat, fish, eggs or dried beans (if vegetarian); 200mL milk or equivalent in cheese or yoghurt; and one tablespoon butter, margarine or oil.

2 Maintain a healthy body weight, one which is neither too fat nor too thin.

3 Cut back on fats by reducing oil, cream, fried foods, pastries, biscuits, snack foods, fatty meats and high-fat cheese.

4 Eat more fibre from grains, vegetables, legumes (beans and lentils), fruit and nuts. Soluble fibre, found in oats, rice, fruit and vegetables, can assist in lowering cholesterol, while the insoluble fibre of wheat bran and whole wheat foods helps prevent constipation and bowel disease.

5 Eat more complex carbohydrates by including more pasta, bread, cereals, legumes and vegetables in your daily meals.

6 Limit salt at the table and in cooking. Buy low-salt products such as bread, margarine, butter and canned foods. Cut down on salt gradually and you will not miss the salty taste after three or four weeks.

7 If you drink alcohol, drink it in moderation, which means no more than one or two standard drinks a day. (A standard drink is a glass of wine, a 60 mL glass of sherry, a 300 mL glass of beer or a nip of spirits.)

8 Calcium is essential for strong bones. Low-fat milk, cheese and yoghurt are the richest calcium sources but sardines and salmon with the bones, sesame seeds, prawns, broccoli and nuts provide some. Calcium tablets are recommended for those who do not eat dairy products.

9 Iron, required for healthy blood, is found in lean meats, especially liver, whole grains and bread, dried beans, spinach and other green vegetables. This mineral is often in short supply in women's diets.

10 Rely on food, not vitamin pills. The vitamins in food are in a readily absorbed form and, correctly combined with each other, are difficult to overdose on. Use supplements only under specific circumstances.

USEFUL INFORMATION

		30g	60g	125g	250g
Almonds	ground or slivered	$1/4$ cup	$1/2$ cup	1 cup	2 cups
Apricots	dried, chopped	$1/4$ cup	$1/2$ cup	1 cup	2 cups
Breadcrumbs	dry	$1/4$ cup	$1/2$ cup	1 cup	2 cups
	fresh	$1/2$ cup	1 cup	2 cups	4 cups
Biscuit crumbs		$1/4$ cup	$1/2$ cup	1 cup	2 cups
Butter		$1\frac{1}{2}$ tbsp	$1/4$ cup	$1/2$ cup	1 cup
Cheese	lightly packed, grated	$1/4$ cup	$1/2$ cup	1 cup	2 cups
	Parmesan	$1/4$ cup	$1/2$ cup	1 cup	2 cups
Cherries	glace, chopped	2 tbsp	$1/3$ cup	$3/4$ cup	$1\frac{1}{2}$ cups
Cocoa		$1/4$ cup	$1/2$ cup	1 cup	2 cups
Coconut	desiccated	$1/3$ cup	$2/3$ cup	$1\frac{1}{3}$ cups	$2\frac{2}{3}$ cups
Cornflour		3 tbsp	$1/2$ cup	1 cup	2 cups
Currants		2 tbsp	$1/3$ cup	$2/3$ cup	$1\frac{1}{3}$ cups
Flour	plain and self-raising	$1/4$ cup	$1/2$ cup	1 cup	2 cups
	wholemeal	$1/4$ cup	$1/2$ cup	1 cup	2 cups
Fruit	dried, mixed	2 tbsp	$1/3$ cup	$3/4$ cup	$1\frac{1}{2}$ cups
Nuts	chopped	$1/4$ cup	$1/2$ cup	1 cup	2 cups
Peel	candied	2 tbsp	$1/3$ cup	$3/4$ cup	$1\frac{1}{2}$ cups
Rice	short grain, raw	2 tbsp	$1/4$ cup	$2/3$ cup	$1\frac{1}{4}$ cups
	long grain, raw	2 tbsp	$1/3$ cup	$3/4$ cup	$1\frac{1}{2}$ cups
Rolled Oats		$1/3$ cup	$2/3$ cup	$1\frac{1}{3}$ cups	$2\frac{2}{3}$ cups
Sugar	white or caster	$1\frac{1}{2}$ tbsp	$1/4$ cup	$1/2$ cup	1 cup
	brown or icing	2 tbsp	$1/3$ cup	$3/4$ cup	$1\frac{1}{2}$ cups

Ingredients And COOKING TERMS

ABALONE: A large mollusc with a firm flesh which is available frozen or canned. Drained canned clams could be substituted.

ALFALFA SPROUTS: Seeds that have been germinated and allowed to grow for a few days.

BASTE: To moisten meat or vegetables with raw juices during cooking.

BEAN SPROUTS: Germinated seeds usually from mung or soy beans.

BEETROOT: Regular round beet.

BICARBONATE OF SODA: Baking soda.

BLANCH: Drop food into a pan of boiling water. Return to the boil, then drain immediately and refresh under cold running water to stop the cooking and to retain the colour.

BLENDING: Mixing a liquid such as water into a dry ingredient such as cornflour. The mixture should be smooth, lump free and well combined.

BOIL: Heating a liquid until the surface is bubbling all over.

BREADCRUMBS:
Fresh: One or two day old bread made into crumbs.
Packaged: Use commercially packaged breadcrumbs.

BUTTERNUT PUMPKIN: Butternut squash.

CABBAGE: Savoy, common garden variety.

CANNED TOMATO PIECES: Canned chopped tomatoes.

CAPSICUM: Red or green bell peppers.

CHEESE, TASTY: A firm good-tasting cheddar cheese.

CHICKEN MARYLANDS: Chicken leg joints.

CHILLI SAUCE: Consists of chillies, salt and vinegar. Use sparingly to suit taste.

COCONUT MILK: Available canned or as an instant powder. May be made at home by dissolving 50 g creamed coconut in boiling water.

CORNED BEEF: Salt beef.

CORNFLOUR: Cornstarch, substitute arrowroot.

CRACKED BLACK PEPPERCORNS: Coarsely ground black pepper.

CREAM: Light pouring cream.

CREAMING: Beat together chopped shortening and essence or flavouring until the mixture is as white as possible. Then gradually beat in sugar until the mixture is light and fluffy

ESSENCE: Extract.

FIVE SPICE POWDER: A mixture of ground spices which include cinnamon, cloves, fennel, star anise and Szechuan pepper.

FOLDING IN: Combine ingredients quickly and gently, without deflating what is usually a light mixture. A large metal spoon is ideal for doing this.

FRUIT MINCE: Mincemeat.

GARAM MASALA: Made up of cardamon, cinnamon, cloves, coriander, cumin and nutmeg, often used in Indian cooking.

GINGER:
Fresh: ginger root.
Preserved ginger: root ginger cooked in syrup.

GOLDEN SYRUP: Substitute honey.

GREEN SHALLOTS: Spring onions or scallions.

HOISING SAUCE: Chinese barbecue sauce.

KNEAD: This is usually done on a lightly floured board or bench, the hands or fingertips are used to turn the outside edge of a mixture into the centre. Do this to either shape a mixture into a ball (pastry) or alter the nature of the mixture by working it with your hands (bread dough).

KUMERA: Orange coloured sweet potato.

LEMON BUTTER: Lemon curd or lemon cheese.

MACADAMIA NUTS: A native to Australia, available in cans or packets, may be replaced by Brazil nuts.

MUSTARD, WHOLEGRAIN: A French style of textured mustard with crushed mustard seeds.

OYSTER SAUCE: A rich brown bottled sauce made from oysters cooked in salt and soy sauce.

PORK FILLETS: Skinless, boneless eye fillet from the loin.

PUREE: Push fresh or cooked food through a sieve or strainer to make a smooth mixture. Alternatively you can use the food processor to puree.

READY ROLLED PUFF OR SHORT-CRUST PASTRY: Use just-thawed frozen puff or shortcrust pastry rolled out to required size.

RIB EYE STEAK: Sirloin steak.

ROCKMELON: Use cantaloupe melon.

SEGMENT: Cut the peel and all white pith from citrus fruit, then cut between membranes joining segments.

SHALLOTS: Vegetables with small white bulbs and long green leaves. Substitute spring onion or onion.

SIMMER: Heating a liquid until the surface has the odd bubble bursting through.

SNAPPER: A warm water sea fish with a delicate white flesh. Substitute sea bream.

SNOW PEAS: Mangetout peas.

SOUR CREAM: Commercially soured cream.

SOY SAUCE: Made from fermented soya beans.

STOCK: Homemade gives best result. For convenience, substitute one stock cube for every two cups water.

THREE BEAN MIX: Canned mixed beans.

TOASTING NUTS: Spread the nuts evenly on an oven tray. Bake at 180°C for 5-8 minutes or until lightly browned.

TOFU: Made from boiled, crushed soya beans; easily digested, highly nutritious.

TOMATO PASTE: Tomato puree.

VEAL SCHNITZELS: Veal escalopes.

VEGETABLE EXTRACT: Made of vegetable protein extract, yeast, spices and usually has added vitamins.

WHITE FISH: Non-oily fish such as whiting, plaice or ling.

WHITE VINEGAR: Distilled malt vinegar.

ZUCCHINI: Courgette.

INDEX